Godden

The Sound of English

Published by Pronunciation Studio Ltd. 2012
1 Euston Road, London, NW1 2SA
www.pronunciationlondon.co.uk

ISBN 978-0-9573836-0-9

www.thesoundofenglish.org

Please download the full audio by following this link:

www.thesoundofenglish.org/Free/A1b4u78k.zip

Index

Introduction

English is a confusing language to pronounce. With its 19 vowels, 25 consonants, weak forms, linking and intonation it poses plenty of problems to the non-native speaker. Not to forget the way its written form is so dramatically different from its pronunciation.

'The Sound of English' takes you step by step through these tricky areas, covering the sounds, structures and melodies of English in a logical way. Through studying the course you will learn:

+ How to pronounce every vowel and consonant sound of English.
+ Correct use of stress and intonation.
+ The rules of joining and sound selection.
+ To listen with accuracy to English speech.
+ Phonetic symbols for all the sounds of English.

The course will show you how to experience English as a native does: instinctively through listening and sound production.

The course and book were designed, written and recorded through years of teaching experience at the Pronunciation Studio speech school in London. The method is modern and user-friendly, based on introducing, drilling and exercising all the key areas to gradually build students' confidence and knowledge.

As you go through the course you can download extra materials and read tips on the course website: www.thesoundofenglish.org. You will also find useful information about teachers and contact information if you have any questions.

We hope you enjoy the course, let us know how you get on with improving your English pronunciation!

Joseph Hudson

Author & Teacher
The Sound of English

How to Use the Book

Every chapter is split into the following sections:

- **Sounds**: how to pronounce vowels and consonants.
- **Sound Comparison**: focus on difficult sounds that are often confusing.
- **Spelling & Sound**: how to turn written English into speech.
- **Structure**: how English joins together and the weak/strong structure.
- **Intonation**: the use of pitch and stress in speech.

Most activities come with audio files to practise with. These are indicated with the following symbol in the left margin: 9.3🎧

Every page of the course contains up to three parts: **NOTES**, **EXERCISES** and **DRILLS** as follows:

NOTES

> ✦ All notes appear in **grey boxes** like this one.
> ✦ Here you will find the **rules and production notes** for each section.

EXERCISES

- Complete the exercises and check your answers with the audio or answer key.
- The answer key is found in the back of the book on pages 113-130.

DRILLS

- Repeat drills regularly with the recording until they become easy to produce.
- There is space on the recordings to repeat after each sentence or sound.

EXTRA MATERIALS & CLASSES

- Many of the exercises in 'The Sound of English' have extra practice activities available to download from our website, visit: www.thesoundofenglish.org
- You can also find information about where to study the course with qualified teachers on the website.

IPA Chart

- IPA is **phonetic script**, it shows us the sounds to pronounce rather than spelling.
- The script is very useful for improving accuracy in pronunciation.
- You will learn each sound and its possible spellings on the course.

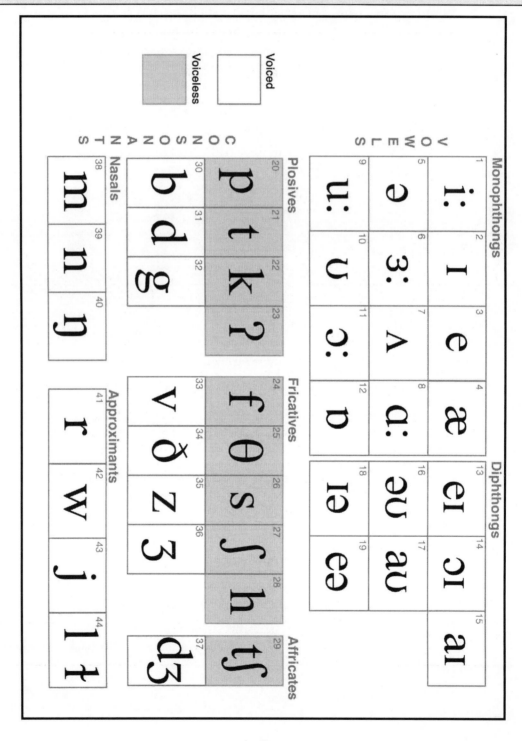

Chapter 1

Sounds	– Consonants – Vowels	
Spelling & Sound	'ghoti' Schwa	*ghoti*
Structure	Function & Content	
Intonation	Patterns Usage	
Postscript	IPA	/ˈpɜːsənli/
		Answer Key Pages 113-114

Consonant Types | Sound

> * Consonant sounds are produced by **blocking air** as it leaves the mouth.
> * This course shows you how to pronounce all **25 consonant sounds** of English.
> * Below is an example of each consonant sound - listen and read them.

1.1 🎧

Type of Sound	Sound	Example 1	Example 2
plosive (complete block of air followed by explosion)	p	pin	cap
	b	bag	robe
	t	time	late
	d	door	feed
	k	cash	sock
	g	girl	flag
	ʔ	-	football
fricative (constant flow of air "squeezed" through a block, sounds like friction)	f	full	knife
	v	vest	cave
	θ	think	earth
	ð	those	bathe
	s	sight	kiss
	z	zoo	nose
	ʃ	shirt	crash
	ʒ	-	pleasure
	h	high	-
affricate (plosive followed by fricative)	tʃ	chose	catch
	dʒ	joy	stage
nasal (air is released through the nose)	m	mood	calm
	n	now	turn
	ŋ	-	bang
approximant (vowel-like consonant, no full block of air occurs)	w	wall	-
	j	yellow	-
	r	room	-
	l / ɫ	law	pill

Consonant Articulation | Sound

> - We use the articulators: **tongue**, **lips**, & **teeth**, to block air.
> - The **places** where we block air in English are shown below.

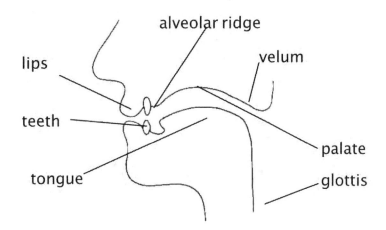

EXERCISE

- Listen to the recording and match the sounds in the boxes with their articulation diagrams (the first one has been done). The arrows point to the place of articulation.

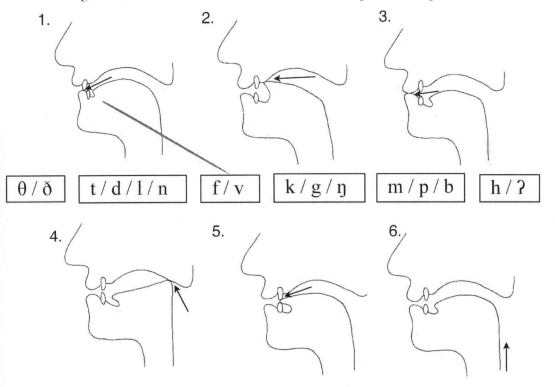

1.   2.   3.

| θ / ð | t / d / l / n | f / v | k / g / ŋ | m / p / b | h / ? |

4.   5.   6.

- Check your answers in the answer key on page 112.

Vowels | Sounds

- ✦ A neutral English accent has **19 vowel sounds**.
- ✦ There are 3 types of English vowel sound - **short**, **long** and **diphthong**.
- ✦ **English spelling** does not always show us which sound to pronounce.
- ✦ We will learn how to pronounce each individual vowel sound on this course.

1.3 🎧

Type of Sound	Sound	Spellings	Examples
short (single mouth position)	ə	a, e, o, u	alive, the, today, supply
	ɪ	i	thin, sit, rich
	ʊ	u, oo, ou	put, look, should
	e	e, ea, ie	went, bread, friend
	ʌ	u, o	fun, love, money
	æ	a	cat, hand, fan
	ɒ	o, a	rob, top, watch
long (single mouth position)	iː	ee, ea	need, beat, team
	uː	ew, oo, o_e	few, boot, lose
	ɜː	ir, ur, wor	third, turn, worse
	ɔː	al, aw, or, our, oor	talk, law, port
	ɑː	a, al, ar	glass, half, car
diphthong (double mouth position)	eɪ	ay, ea, ae, ai	pay, great, maid
	ɔɪ	oi, oy	noise, toy, choice
	aɪ	ie, i_e, i, y	fine, like, might
	əʊ	o, o_e, oa	no, stone, road
	aʊ	ou, ow	round, how, brown
	ɪə	eer, ear	beer, hear, steer
	eə	are, ere, ea, ai	care, there, bear

Vowel Articulation | Sounds

- A vowel sound is made by **shaping the mouth** as air flows out.
- Articulators used to shape the mouth are: **tongue**, **lips** and **jaw**.
- The chart below shows examples of mouth positions in English.

Example	Position		
	tongue	**lips**	**jaw**
i: (keep)	front	spread	close
3: (bird)	mid	relaxed	mid
ɒ (watch)	back	rounded	open

DRILL

- Repeat the following sentences. Notice your jaw opening each time.

1. Keep this red bag.   2. Who took Paul's watch?   3. The bird runs fast.

- Which sentence contains only rounded vowels?

Introduction | Spelling & Sound

1.6 🎧
- English spelling does not always indicate pronunciation.
- It was famously claimed that the word 'fish' could be spelt 'ghoti' because:

'gh' in 'enough' is pronounced /f/

'o' in 'women' is pronounced /ɪ/

'ti' in 'motion' is pronounced /ʃ/

so 'ghoti' could be pronounced /fɪʃ/!

ghoti

---

* The pronunciation of many English sounds **can be predicted** by their spelling.
* The **'Spelling & Sound'** section shows you how to select sounds accurately by interpreting spelling.

EXERCISE

- Each group of words contains an identical spelling.
- Circle the word that you think is **pronounced** differently from the others.

1. goose   loose   (choose)
2. nose   rose   lose
3. played   stopped   liked
4. father   author   Northern
5. paid   maid   said
6. put   but   hut
7. none   done   gone
8. foot   book   food
9. slow   now   cow
10. word   work   worn
11. watch   wall   was

1.7 🎧   - Listen and check your answers.

Schwa | Spelling & Sound

- Match the words below with the IPA transcription on the right:

8 🎧

Word	IPA Transcription
around	ˈmænə
manner	ˈseɪlə
sailor	ˈkæktəs
cactus	əˈraʊnd

- Which sound appears in every IPA transcription?

9 🎧

+ The schwa sound /ə/ can be spelt as < a >, < e >, < o > and < u >.
+ The schwa is the **most common vowel sound** in English.
+ The schwa is **weak** - it can never be stressed.
+ The production of the schwa is **neutral**: lips, jaw and tongue are **relaxed**

EXERCISE

- Every word in the box below contains one schwa sound.
- Listen to the recording and underline the schwa in each word.

0 🎧

servant persist bacon picture commit alive
jumper sublime London salad Peru structure
suggest soldier persuade combine balloon
terror cushion scripture tighten sofa Russia

- Think of any word in English with 3 syllables or more.
- How many schwa sounds does it contain? Check in a dictionary.

EXAMPLE: 'conspiracy' = 2 schwa sounds.

Function & Content | Structure

- Listen to the sentence below:

1.11 🎧   "Shall we go for a walk?"

- Which words are stressed? Why?

✦ Spoken English is divided into function and content words.

✦ **Function words** carry only grammatical meaning, such as:

Word Type	Examples
prepositions	to from for of with by
auxiliaries	are was do have could would shall can
articles	a an the
quantifiers	some any few all
pronouns	he she it you I this that

✦ **Content words** carry real meaning such as:

Word Type	Examples
nouns	car wedding James table joy
verbs	move drink turn enjoy think
adjectives	big interesting quiet slow bright
adverbs	quickly quietly fortunately often again

EXERCISE

- In the sentences below, <u>underline</u> the function words:

1.12 🎧
1. Can we go for a swim in the sea?
2. It's a beautiful day in the South of England.
3. How do you want to pay for this, sir?
4. Jessica Smith is required in 'Arrivals' immediately.
5. When you get to the station, give me a call.
6. Would you like some of my carrot cake?

- Read and listen to the passage below, the schwa sound is written in IPA:

I'd like tə go shopping fər ə pair əf shoes, bət thə shops ə closed becəse thəs ə weathər ələrt. əparrəntly lots əf snow is coming in frəm thə Highlənds so thə govərnmənt həv ədvised peopəl tə stay ət home.

- Which function words are pronounced with a schwa sound in the passage?

- ◆ Many function words are pronounced with schwa **when they are weak.**
- ◆ If a function word is **stressed**, it **can not be pronounced with schwa.**
- ◆ Function words are always **strong** when said **alone.**

DRILL

- Say the word on the left alone (strong), then say it in the sentence on the right using the schwa sound (weak):

Word (STRONG)	Sentence (WEAK)
1	to /tu:/	I went **to** work early. /tə/
2	are /ɑː/	What **are** you doing? /ə/
3	was /wɒz/	**Was** it warm in Greece? /wəz/
4	from /frɒm/	This card's **from** my family. /frəm/
5	there /ðeə/	**There** weren't enough drinks. /ðə/
6	can /kæn/	Where **can** we buy a map? /kən/
7	her /hɜː/	**Her** car's broken down. /hə/
8	for /fɔː/	I'll repeat **for** the last time! /fə/

Introduction | Intonation

- Listen to the following question being answered in three different ways:

1.15

A Johnny, have you finished your homework?

    1. ↘Yes
B 2. ↘↗Yes
    3. ↗Yes

- Which answer (B) means i) maybe ii) definitely iii) why are you asking me?

- Spoken English uses 3 intonation patterns - **fall**, **fall-rise** & **rise**.
- Intonation shows us the **speaker's attitude** to what they are saying.

DRILL

- Repeat after the recording:

1.16

1. a)↘Yes b)↘↗Yes c)↗Yes
2. a)↘No b)↘↗No c)↗No

EXERCISE

- Listen to the conversations and circle the answer you hear:

1.17

1. Are you married?   Yes↘ ↘↗ ↗
2. Did you enjoy the film?   Yes ↘ ↘↗ ↗
3. Can you afford this meal? Yes ↘ ↘↗ ↗
4. You're drunk, aren't you? No ↘ ↘↗ ↗
5. Is this your first class?   No ↘ ↘↗ ↗
6. Did you eat all the chocolate? No ↘ ↘↗ ↗

Usage | Intonation

+ Intonation shows us a speakers' **attitude** to their words.
+ This course will show you **how to produce English intonation** in your speech.
+ Some important examples of intonation usage are displayed below.

EXERCISE

1. ATTITUDE

- Listen to the following conversation twice:

8 A "Dad, I've got some news, I'm getting married¡"
B "Excellent"

i) How is the father's reaction different in each case?
ii) How does he show this with intonation?

2. IMPLICATION

- Listen to the following conversation twice:

9 A "What did you think of the film?"   B "It was good."

i) What is the difference in meaning between the two versions?
ii) How is the intonation in the word 'good' different the second time?

3. REPETITION

Listen to the following conversation:

20 A "Who are you meeting tonight?"   B "Nicole Kidman"."
A "Who are you meeting tonight?"   B "Not the Nicole Kidman¡"

- Person A says the same question twice, but the intonation is different the second time.
How does it change and why?

IPA | Postscript

- Look at the dictionary entry for the word "personally":

personally   /ˈpɜːsənli/

- What differences do you notice between the spelt and the IPA versions?

> + IPA **(International Phonetic Alphabet)** shows the **way we pronounce words**.
> + In English, the pronunciation of a word often differs from its spelling, making IPA a **very useful study tool** to improve your pronunciation.
> + **Stress** is marked in IPA using the following symbol / ˈ/

EXERCISE

i) Write the words from the box below into the chart next to their IPA transcription.

ii) Write the silent consonant from each word into the 3rd column.

cupboard island half often write know light lamb handbag autumn

	Word	IPA	Silent Consonant(s)
1	autumn	ˈɔːtəm	n
2	half	hɑːf	l
3		læm	
4		nəʊ	
5		ˈaɪlənd	
6		laɪt	
7		ˈkʌbəd	
8		raɪt	
9		ˈɒfən	
10		ˈhænbæg	

1.21 🎧   - Listen to the recording to check your answers and practise saying the words.

15

Chapter 2

Sounds	Fricative Consonants	f v θ ð s z ʃ ʒ
Sound Comparison	θ vs ð	
Spelling & Sound	⟨ s ⟩ Endings	
Structure	Schwa Function Words	
Intonation	Sentence Stress	
Postscript	Homographs	
	Answer Key Pages 115-116	

- Fricatives are made by **squeezing air** between two articulators.
- There are **9 fricative consonant sounds** in English (see chapter 5 for /h/):

Sound	Spellings / Examples	Position
f	< f, gh, ph > fee food first face phone beef roof laugh rough loft free flute fright flower	teeth + lip
V	< v > video vet van vote vow leave move serve love pave drove wives knives of*	
θ	< th > third thought thing thumb theory tooth worth path myth cloth month maths athlete health	tongue + teeth
ð	< th > these that other there the smooth bathe although clothes mouths rhythm	
s	< s, c, x > seed soup certain said south worse force case nice mouse first past risk fax	alveolar
z	< z, s > zoo zip zone cheese lose Mars buzz because lazy size rose design	
ʃ	< sh, ch, ti, s > sheet shoe ship sugar champagne show marsh Welsh rush cash sanction patient station	post-alveolar
ʒ	< s, g > explosion Peugeot usual collage Asia measure vision	

2.1

* 'of' is the only word in English spelt with < f > and pronounced /v/.

DRILL

f

Fred and Fiona **ph**oned Fred's ne**ph**ew in **F**inland on **F**riday.

I **f**eel **f**abulously **f**it, laughed Al**f**red at **F**arnham **f**ood **f**estival.

θ

Thanks for the **th**eatre. I **th**ought it was **th**rilling.

Ca**th**y's me**th**ods as an or**th**odontist **th**oroughly **th**rash her me**th**ods as a philan**th**ropist.

---

s

I must **s**ay, it'**s** been **s**o fabulou**s s**taying in **s**uch **s**plendid **s**urroundings.

Tonight'**s s**upper is a choi**ce**: **s**ea ba**ss** or a **s**alad **s**andwich.

∫

Sharon **sh**ould **sh**ow more patients in relation to her Wel**sh** relations.

Should **sh**e sell **sh**orts, **sh**irts, fi**sh** and sea **sh**ells in the same **sh**op?

---

v

Valerie drove the deli**v**ery **v**an to Do**v**er then **v**anished to **V**alencia.

Have **V**incent and **V**icky in**v**ited Da**v**id to their ca**v**e?

ð

I ga**th**er **th**at **th**e rhy**th**m of **th**is is Nor**th**ern, ra**th**er **th**an Sou**th**ern.

Don't bo**th**er with o**th**er pa**th**s, **th**is one's fur**th**er but smoo**th**er **th**an **th**e others.

---

z

The**se** lazy boo**z**ers spend their day**s** do**s**ing in a ha**z**e - I'm ama**z**ed.

A**s** long a**s Z**ack remain**s** in this busine**ss** I won't re**s**ign.

ʒ

Did they mea**s**ure the corro**s**ion after the explo**s**ion in A**s**ia.

Peugeot'**s** vi**s**ion is unu**s**ual A**s**ian expo**s**ure.

< th > | Sound Comparison

- Listen carefully to the two < th > sounds pronounced 4 times each:

2.3 🎧

$$_1. \theta \quad _2. \eth$$

- What differences are there between the two sounds?

_____

EXERCISE

- Listen to the words in the box below and write them into the correct column in the chart according to the pronunciation of < th >:

2.4 🎧

South Southern both thought this the thank those bathe bath baths fifths rather author mouths mouth months soothe	
/θ/	/ð/
South	*Southern*

Check your answers before continuing.

- In the notes, write an example for each rule from the table above:

RULES	EXAMPLES
✦ Most **content words** are pronounced with /θ/	*South, thought*
✦ All **function words** are pronounced with /ð/	_____
✦ Verbs ending < **the** > are pronounced with /ð/	_____
✦ Plural words ending < **vowel + ths** > are pronounced /ð/	_____
✦ Plural words ending < **consonant + ths** > are pronounced /θ/	_____
✦ Words containing < **ther** > are pronounced /ð/	_____

EXCEPTIONS

✦ **Plurals pronounced /θ/**: deaths, moths, cloths.
✦ **Content words pronounced /ð/**: smooth, rhythm.
✦ **'with'** and its derivatives (withdraw, within etc.) can be pronounced /θ/ or /ð/.

EXERCISE

- Circle the odd word out in each line:

1. month   mouth   (mouths)   moth   mathematics
2. father   brother   author   heather   further
3. thought   healthy   those   atheist   throw
4. months   births   clothes   sevenths   widths
5. this   that   the   thin   them

EXERCISE

"Go from start to finish **only** on voiced /ð/ squares. You can only move vertically and horizontally, **NOT** diagonally."

START

theory	bother	author	cloth	faith	birth
North	breathe →	these	leather	athlete	both
South	thing	earth	father	breath	seventh
bath	thought	ninth	Southern	nothing	thousand
teeth	together	those	other	catholic	maths
feather	rhythm	theatre	death	threat	path
although	eighth	tooth	myth	anthology	ninth

FINISH

20

< s > **Endings** | Spelling & Sound

- Listen to the following sentence:

2.6 🎧   **Why's Matt's** son wearing those **badges**?

- How is the < s > at the end of each **bold** word pronounced?
- Why has the < s > been added to each word?

When we add an < s > to a word (root), the following pronunciation rule applies:

2.7 🎧   ✦ Root words ending in voiceless sounds + < s > will be pronounced /s/:
     EXAMPLES: bits, shops, wants

    ✦ Root words ending in voiced sounds + < s > will be pronounced /z/:
     EXAMPLES: shoes, things, ways

    ✦ Root words ending in: /s, z, ʃ, ʒ, tʃ, dʒ/ + < s > will be pronounced /ɪz/:
     EXAMPLES: faces, watches, cages

DRILL

2.8 🎧

Root ends with:	Example	+ s	<s> sound	IPA
voiceless sound	cap	caps	/s/	/kæps/
	state	states		/steɪts/
	tank	tanks		/tæŋks/
	laugh	laughs		/lɑːfs/
	what	what's		/wɒts/
voiced sound	star	stars	/z/	/stɑːz/
	rub	rubs		/rʌbz/
	mug	mugs		/mʌgz/
	show	shows		/ʃəʊz/
	gather	gathers		/gæðəz/
/s, z, ʃ, ʒ, tʃ, dʒ/	miss	misses	/ɪz/	/mɪsɪz/
	lose	loses		/luːzɪz/
	push	pushes		/pʊʃɪz/
	match	matches		/mætʃɪz/
	badge	badges		/bædʒɪz/

EXERCISE

- Using the audio file, add an < s > to the words in the box, then place them in the correct column according to their pronunciation.

top hand choose lob tank beg miss return fax want chase laugh surf love create answer amaze pray alert push inch prefer match seem age look climb badge crack interest		
/s/	/z/	/ɪz/
tops	hands	chooses

- Check your answers and practise saying the words.

EXERCISE

- Circle the odd word out in each line:

1. draws stars employs requires (devastates)

2. raids lobs traces bugs remembers

3. invests sacks maps fails coughs

4. houses mashes rages passes drags

5. aims fails shelters grills talks

6. places stores tears retires alludes

- Check your answers and practise saying the words.

Schwa | Structure

- Listen carefully to the sentence:

2.11 🎧   **'There are a few of them.'**

- How many schwa vowel sounds were pronounced?

> ✦ Function words are **normally weak** in pronunciation.
> ✦ Many function words are **pronounced with a schwa** when they are weak.

DRILL

- Repeat **at the same time as the recording** using the schwa vowel sound for every word then clapping your hands on the ⊙ symbol:

2.12 🎧

1. ⊙ to ⊙ a ⊙ the ⊙ some ⊙
2. ⊙ are ⊙ were ⊙ was ⊙ have ⊙
3. ⊙ that ⊙ shall ⊙ and ⊙ would ⊙
4. ⊙ her ⊙ there ⊙ for ⊙ from ⊙
5. ⊙ do ⊙ does ⊙ can ⊙ but ⊙

EXERCISE

- Listen to the sentences and write the missing words in. All missing words are weak function words pronounced with schwa:

2.13 🎧

1. ____ ____ parents coming ____ ____ show?
2. ____ we buy ____ chocolate ____ Margaret?
3. ____ ____ ____ card ____ Claire today.
4. ____ we meet ____ dinner in ____ bar?
5. What ____ I done ____ ____ dinner?
6. ____ you ____ I ask ____?
7. ____ they think ____ we will?

23

Stressed Function Words | Structure

- Function words **are not pronounced with schwa** if they are:

   1. Stressed due to meaning.

   EXAMPLE: A Is that present from David?
                  B No, it's *for* David!

   2. At the end of the sentence/unit:

   EXAMPLE: A Who's the present <u>for</u>?
                  B It's for John.

EXERCISE

- In the following sentences, circle the bold words **if they are pronounced with schwa:**

1. to   A Come on! It's time to go **to** school!
            B Oh, but mum, do I have **to**?

2. from   A Where are you **from**?
              B I'm **from** Poland.

3. for   A Is this card **for** me?
             B I don't know who it's **for**.

4. are   A Kevin and Julie **are** getting married!
             B **Are** they! How charming.

5. was   A **Was** Geoffrey at the lecture last night?
             B Yes I think he **was**.

6. were   A If I **were** you, I'd find another job.
              B I would if there **were** any other jobs

7. some   A I've got **some** belgian chocolate here!
              B Oooo - can I have **some**!.

8. can   A **Can** anyone help me carry these bags?
             B I **can**!

9. her   A Sarah seems really upset! What did you say to **her**?
             B I only told **her** to talk more quietly!

- Practise saying the conversations with the recording.

Sentence Stress | Intonation

- Listen to the following exchange.

2.16 🎧

A "What would you like?"
B "A cup of tea"

- Which words are stressed?
- Of the stressed words, which words are strongest?

+ In spoken English we **stress content words**.
+ **One word in every sentence** is more stressed than the others.
+ Normally the **last content word** is the most stressed word.

EXERCISE

- Match the content words on the left with the content words on the right.

	pair			beef
	pint			bread
	leg			poems
	bunch			wine
a	bag	of		shoes
	glass			milk
	book			flowers
	joint			lamb
	loaf			crisps

DRILL

- Repeat the rhythm followed by each sentence from the exercise:

2.17 🎧

. X . X

. x . X | a pair of shoes

Tonic Syllable | Intonation

- Listen to the conversation and decide which word is most stressed in each sentence:

A "Did you buy anything?"

        B "I wasn't going to...."

A "So what's in the bag?"

        B "A pair of trousers."

> ✦ **One word** carries more stress than the others in all sentences.
> ✦ This stressed word is called the '**tonic syllable**'.
> ✦ Normally the tonic syllable is found in the **last content word** of the sentence.

EXERCISE

- Circle the content words in the box below:

four	to	two	some	are	art	wife	half
would	us	use	something	sum	she	sheet	
	anything	sorting	with	wood			

- Underline the tonic syllable in the last content word of these sentences:

1. What do you <u>want</u> from me?
2. You make me laugh.
3. Shall we give it to him?
4. I think she wanted something.
5. I'd certainly like you to.
6. It's always so lovely to see them.
7. Can I have some?
8. Who's this card for.
9. What a waste of time and money.
10. We used to have so much fun there.

9 - Listen and repeat the sentences placing a strong stress on the tonic.

Homographs | Postscript

- Read the following two sentences:

2.20 🎧   "What on earth am I going to /ri:d/ this summer holiday?"
            "Have you /red/ "Wolf Hall"? It's brilliant!"

- How are the 2 words in IPA written in English?

◆ Homographs are words that are **spelt the same** but **pronounced differently**.

EXERCISE

- For each pair of sentences, write the homograph represented by the words in IPA:

1. a) What time does the shop /kləʊz/?   *close*

b) Jill and Geoffrey have been /kləʊs/ friends since childhood.

2. a) It's rare to find /led/ in piping or pencils these days.

b) "Cambridge have taken the /li:d/ and look certain to win."   _____

3. a) Think of any /nʌmbə/ between 1 and 10.

b) Yes, my mouth feels a bit /nʌmə/ with the anaesthetic.   _____

4. a) I must admit, a /tɪə/ came to my eye at the end of 'Titanic'.

b) This certificate is worthless, I might as well /teə/ it up.   _____

5. a) There's quite a /wɪnd/ blowing from the North today.

b) Johnny, don't /waɪnd/ your sister up like that!   _____

6. a) For this chart, you need 3 columns and 5 /rəʊz/.

b) Our neighbours are always having /raʊz/ about money.   _____

2.21 🎧   - Check your answers in the key then listen to the sentences.

27

Chapter 3

Sounds	Long Vowels	iː uː ɜː ɔː ɑː
Sound Comparison	ɪ vs iː	
Spelling & Sound	Silent ⟨ r ⟩	
Structure	2 Syllable Words	
Intonation	Wh–Questions	
Postscript	Homophones	
		Answer Key Pages 117-118

Long Vowels | Sounds

3.1 🎧   - What do British English speakers say when they are thinking?

> + Spoken English contains **5 long vowel sounds**.
> + Each long vowel uses **one unique position of the mouth**.
> + Every long vowel sound has **several possible spellings**.

Sound	Spellings	Examples	Mouth Position		
			Tongue	Lips	Jaw
i:	ee ea ei/ie	feet, sheep leave, easy, beach receive, achieve	front	spread	close
u:	ew oo ou ue	new, grew, few boot, food, shoot soup, route glue, Sue	back	rounded	close
ɜ:	ir ur wor	shirt, sir, bird turn, murder, curl word, world, worse	flat	relaxed	mid
ɔ:	al aw or/our/oor	talk, hall saw, raw, law short, four, poor	back	rounded	mid
ɑ:	a al ar	glass, pass, fast calm, palm dark, farm	flat	relaxed	open

3.2 🎧

29

EXERCISE

- Place the words in the box into the correct column below:

Tuesday jaw curse dream half park clue cheek word spoon grief walk father suit Chinese horse thirty last evening church door food shark earth brought quarter threw car worth beast

i:	u:	ɜ:	ɔ:	ɑ:
	Tuesday			

3 🎧 - Listen to the words, then check your answers in the key.

DRILL

- Repeat the absurd sentences, paying attention to the long vowel sounds:

4 🎧

i:

Cheap sheets and eating cheese can besiege one's sleep.
I dreamed of sheep, sleeping in the fields near Stevenage.

u:

It's truly a beautiful route from Waterloo to London Zoo.
Is this food new to you? It's a Sudanese stew!

ɜ:

Burt the bird and Curt the worm are on the worst possible terms.
That was the first service I've heard in church with Shirley.

ɔ:

At a quarter to four we'll call Mr Ball's daughter in Cornwall.
Four walls, one door and a floor, no more.

ɑ:

I can't laugh at Charles Darwin's masterpiece, it's too hard.
Half a banana tart, a Mars bar and a large glass of lager please.

30

ɪ vs iː | **Sound Comparison**

- Listen carefully to the following 2 sentences:

3.5 🎧

> "**Sit** down!"
>
> "Please, take a **seat**."

- What do you notice about the different pronunciation of the bold words?

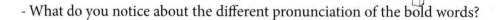

+ There are 2 main differences between the vowel sounds /ɪ/ and /iː/:
  1. The **position of the mouth** (see chart below).
  2. /iː/ is normally (though not always) longer than /ɪ/.
+ /iː/ is **spelt with two vowels** < ee / ei / ie / ea > in written English.
+ /ɪ/ is **spelt as < i >** in written English (except when weak).

	Tongue	Jaw	Lips
ɪ	mid-front	mid-close	relaxed
iː	front	close	spread

Drill

3.6 🎧

	1	2	3	4	5	6	7	8
ɪ	ship	lick	hit	sit	fit	bin	sin	lid
iː	sheep	leak	heat	seat	feet	bean	seen	lead

EXERCISE

- Using the consonant sounds in the left column, create two words, with /ɪ/ then /iː/.
- If you cannot think of the word, use a dictionary or the recording to help.

	Consonants	ɪ	iː
1	d ___ d	*did*	*deed*
2	tʃ ___ p	*chip*	*cheap*
3	r ___ d		
4	f ___ st		
5	___ tʃ		
6	gr ___ n		
7	tʃ ___ k		
8	l ___ v		
9	p ___ k		
10	s ___ k		

7 - Listen to the answers and practise saying the words.

EXERCISE

- Using words from the previous exercise, fill in the gaps:

1. a) I'm having fish and *chip*_s for dinner, do you want some?
   b) £200 for that rusty old thing? Well, it's not *cheap*, is it?

2. a) When I told her, she went _____ with envy.
   b) Stop _____ning! It's not funny.

3. a) Give them £50 _____ and tell them to leave.
   b) If it's a mosquito bite it *will* _____, but don't scratch, it'll make it worse.

4. a) It's over, David, I just want you to _____.
   b) Where does your boyfriend _____, nearby?

5. a) I've got them in red, green and yellow, so take your _____.
   b) The highest _____ in the UK is Ben Nevis at 1344 metres.

6. a) Can you get _____ of this bag of rubbish for me?
   b) Can't you _____? It says 'don't walk on the grass!'

8 - Listen, check and practise your answers.

32

< r > | Spelling & Sound

- Which word below **does not** contain a pronounced /r/?

3.9   bread   butter

+ In British English we do not pronounce every written < r >.
3.10 + If an < r > appears **before a vowel sound**, we pronounce it:
    EXAMPLES: rat, rice, pretty, strain, cry, story

+ If an < r > appears **after a vowel sound**, we do not pronounce it.
    EXAMPLES: car, court, learn, shorter, store

EXERCISE

- Write the correct words underneath the pictures, they contain silent < r >:

1. *heart*

2. _____

3. _____

4. _____

5. _____

6. _____

7. _____

8. _____

9. _____

3.11   - Listen to check your answers.

EXERCISE

- Circle the names that contain a silent < r > sound:

Catherine   Eric   Heather   Shirly

Carla   Mary   Burt   Brenda

Laura   Rachel   Charlotte   Kirsty   Doreen

2 - Listen to check your answers.

EXERCISE

- Move from start to finish by **only going on words that contain silent < r >**.
  You may only move horizontally or vertically, **NOT** diagonally.

START

ray	three	increase	crash	release	father	interest
lorry	treatment	throw	crew	arrive	learn	horse
train	birthday	sharp	sport	harder	Syria	Berlin
warm	water	drill	crisps	important	Turkey	fork
Barcelona	revive	break	Peru	brilliant	Iraq	tray
poor	first	burn	liberal	Brighton	Andrew	grey
poorest	current	perfect	Liverpool	New York	Caroline	terrible
richest	recent	Euro	real	Manchester	foreign	remote

FINISH

3 - Listen to check your route.

34

Two Syllable Words | Structure

- Listen to the conversation:

3.14 🎧   "This **pic**ture is **per**fect!"

"I a**gree**, it's sub**lime**!"

♦ All English words of 2 syllables or more contain **one main stress**.
♦ The main stress may appear on the **first syllable (X .)** or the **second syllable (. X)**.
♦ In IPA, stress is marked with the symbol / ' / **before** the stressed syllable.
EXAMPLES: pur'suit, 'purchase, com'plete, 'common.

DRILL

3.15 🎧

X .   . X

'anthem	a'maze
'beggar	be'lieve
'castle	co'rrupt
'forest	for'give
'England	em'ploy
'noble	po'lite
'question	sub'mit

EXERCISE

- Listen and place the words in the box below into the correct columns according to their stress patterns:

angle alive appeal beside awful bishop balloon carpet father commit foolish decide delete erase forbid pardon involve English candle machine persuade lettuce release orphan revise survive sofa turtle

(X .) 1st Syllable Stress	(. X) 2nd Syllable Stress
angle	*alive*

EXERCISE

- Circle the word that contains a different stress pattern in each line:

1. palate passion (parade) pasta
2. conquer corrupt confess convince
3. able anchor amaze anxious
4. canal candle canon candy
5. master mansion machine marriage
6. police poker pocket ponder

- Check your answers in the answer key.

Wh- Questions | Intonation

- Listen to the question 'where are you going?' in these conversations:

3.17 🎧

1. A I'm going on holiday.
   B **Where are you going?**

2. A I'm going to Antarctica.
   B **Where are you going?**

- How is the intonation different? Why?

> • When we ask for **new information**, we normally use falling ↘ intonation.
> • When we **already know the answer** to a question, we use rising ↗ intonation.
> • In new information questions, we normally **stress the last content word**.
> • In repeated questions , we normally **stress the question word**.

Drill

3.18 🎧

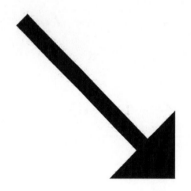

1. ↘Who?
2. ↘Where?
3. ↘Why?
4. When will you get ↘back?
5. Why can't you ↘come?
6. Which one is ↘yours.
7. Where are you ↘going?
8. What are you ↘doing?
9. How ↘much?

3.19 🎧

1. ↗Who?
2. ↗Where?
3. ↗Why?
4. ↗When will you get back?
5. ↗Why can't you come?
6. ↗Which one is yours?
7. ↗Where are you going?
8. ↗What are you doing?
9. ↗How much?

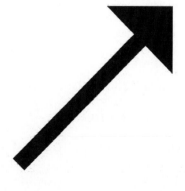

EXERCISE

- Study the conversations and decide from the context if the intonation in the question is falling (new information) or rising (repeated information). Circle the answers:

1
a) I'm meeting Zainab later.
   Who?
b) I'm meeting someone later.
   Who?

2
a) I should be back next year, it depends how my job goes.
   When will you get back?
b) I'm having a great time here, but I'm missing home.
   When will you get back?

3
a) I think I'll have to miss tomorrow's meeting.
   Why can't you come?
b) I can't come out tonight, my hair is too wet. I had to wash it 3 or 4 times.
   Why can't you come?

4
a) Can you pass me my coat?
   Which one is yours?
b) My car's over there, look, it's the blue Rolls Royce!
   Which one is yours?

5
a) I'm at my sister's house.
   What are you doing?
b) I'm having dinner with Queen Elizabeth.
   What are you doing?

6
a) Well, your car was in quite a bad state. That will be £860.00.
   How much?
b) Would you like to buy a ticket for today's match?
   How much?

7
a) The match starts at 10pm.
   Where?
b) The car's in the airport: car park 5, floor 3, space 34e.
   Where?

- Check your answers and practise the conversations with the recording.

Homophones | Postscript

- Listen to the following dialogue:

3.21 🎧

"There /ɑːnt/ any apples left!"

"Ask your /ɑːnt/ Sue to get some – she's going to the shops."

- Which words are written in IPA? How are they spelt in written English?

> • Homophones are words that are **pronounced identically**, but **spelt differently**.

EXERCISE

i) Write the word for the IPA transcription in each sentence:

1. a) Breathe in the wonderful mountain /eə/! _____
   b) Who is the current /eə/ to the Spanish throne? _____

2. a) Jenny, you look so /bɔːd/! I thought you liked learning English. _____
   b) On the /bɔːd/ you can see this week's figures. _____

3. a) /dɪə/ Karen, I have been meaning to write to you for ages. _____
   b) Richmond Park is full of /dɪə/ roaming around. _____

4. a) For the dough, we'll need /flaʊwə/, water and yeast. _____
   b) Put this beautiful /flaʊwə/ by the window in some water. _____

5. a) I like your new /dʒiːnz/, very fashionable! _____
   b) Jane comes from strong /dʒiːnz/ - her mother's 98! _____

3.22 🎧 - Listen to check your answers.

ii) Every IPA transcription in the box below is a homophone. Which two words do they produce in speech?

3.23 🎧

kɔːt fɑːðə nəʊz nʌn səʊ sʌn θruː wɔː wɔːn weðə bɪld wɪtʃ

EXAMPLE: *court / caught*

39

Chapter 4

Sounds	Plosive Consonants	p t k b d g
Sound Comparison	Glottal Stop vs / t /	
Spelling & Sound	‹ ed › Endings	
Structure	3 Syllable Words	
Intonation	Yes / No Questions	
Postscript	Silent Syllables	
		Answer Key Pages 119-120

Plosive Consonants | Sounds

+ Plosives are made by **fully blocking the flow of air** as it leaves the mouth.
+ Sound is produced when the blocked air is released in an **explosion**.
+ There are **6 plosive sounds** in spoken English:

Sound	Spellings / Words	Position
p	< p > piece pence park pond poet pray press speak stop hope sip cup map	bi-labial (both lips)
b	< b > bean best bug born both broke break beautiful blue blow cab herb rob	
t	< t > tea tan turn tough tape try true stay stone art let mate bright hat	alveolar
d	< d > deep done dark date down duty due dry draw bed seed said hard	
k	< c, k, qu > keep kiss cat card came school crown quick scream excite back check duck lock	velar
g	< g > give gas good gone guide gear glue glove grow great bag log dig bug	

4.1

+ In many English accents a seventh plosive - the **glottal stop** is common. This sound is covered later in the chapter.

DRILL

p

Paul and Peter are putting on a party in their apartment.

Stop pretending you can play poker, it's pathetic, you're appalling.

t

Take some time off tomorrow, Terry, you look tired.

Taste these nuts - their texture is terribly interesting.

k

Can you make this car turn corners a bit quicker?

It's quite quiet here in October, but it's chaotic at Christmas.

b

Bill Burns bought a big bag of beef then built a brick barbecue.

Betty was such a beautiful bride, but Ben was a boring best man.

d

Did David drive down to Devon?

Don't be daft! Dracula didn't design London's dungeons!

g

The game's golden goal was gloriously scored by Gary Gavins.

Go and give these gloves to Graham.

ʔ vs t | Sound Comparison

- Listen carefully to the words below and decide which one does not contain a pronounced /t/ sound:

4.3 🎧

foot   football   footer

4.4 🎧
+ When a < t > appears **at the end of a syllable followed by a consonant**, it will normally be replaced with a glottal stop /ʔ/ in spoken English.
+ The glottal stop is produced by **stopping the flow of air in the glottis**.

4.5 🎧

Sound	Spelling / Words	Position
	< t >	glottal
ʔ	deligh̲tful par̲tly sho̲tgun ca̲twalk cat-flap se̲tback	

EXERCISE

1. Recite the monologue 'Water' pronouncing every underlined < t > as a /t/:

4.6 🎧

Water

'All that Katy wan̲ted
After wai̲ting for̲ty minutes
In thir̲ty degree hea̲t
For her naugh̲ty li̲ttle daugh̲ter
Was a li̲ttle bo̲ttle of wa̲ter.'

4.7 🎧   2. Listen to a recording where each underlined < t > in 'Water' is pronounced as /ʔ/:

- Does it sound very different?
- Have you ever heard an English speaker pronounce in this way?
- If so, where were they from?

EXERCISE

- Circle the odd word out in each line of words considering the /t/ and /ʔ/ sounds:

1. outcome pitfall (waiter) thoughtful
2. butter banter bitter butler
3. Scotland Saturn Hotmail Batman
4. conservative atmosphere altogether timetable
5. waterfall meatball notebook lightning

EXERCISE

- Following the rules, circle the correct sound for the < t > in the conversations:

1. not

a) A Who's taken my car keys?
   B **Not** me, I don't drive.
   t l (?)

b) A Thanks for the lift.
   B **Not** at all, it's a pleasure.
   (t) l ?

2. that

a) A Look! Johnny's eaten all the chocolate but left those sandwiches you made for him!
   B **That** boy will be in trouble when he get's home.
   t l ?

b) A Ha ha, look at Mr. Jones, he's so drunk he can't walk straight!
   B **That** isn't funny you know?
   t l ?

3. what

a) A Hello Mandy - long time no see!
   B Keith! **What** are you doing here?
   t l ?

b) A I think John's angry with me.
   B Why, **what** did you say to him?
   t l ?

4. at

a) A What time shall we have dinner?
   B **At** eight?
   t l ?

b) A When's the next train to Birmingham?
   B **At** nine thirty.
   t l ?

5. bit

a) A Do you fancy going for a walk?
   B It's a **bit** cold, isn't it?
   t l ?

b) A What shall we have with our tea?
   B A **bit** of cake?
   t l ?

44

< ed > endings | Spelling & Sound

- Listen to the following sentence:

4.10 🎧   I **chopped** the garlic, **boiled** the potatoes and **roasted** the beef.

- What is the difference in the pronunciation of the < ed > ending in each bold word?

> When we add < ed > to a word (root), the following pronunciation rule applies:
>
> ✦ If the root ends in a **voiceless consonant**, the < ed > ending is pronounced /t/.
>   **EXAMPLE:** cho**pped**
>
> ✦ If the root ends in a **voiced consonant or a vowel**, the < ed > ending is pronounced /d/.
>   **EXAMPLES:** boi**led**
>
> ✦ If the root ends n a **< t > or a < d >**, the ending is pronounced /ɪd/
>   **EXAMPLES:** roas**ted**

DRILL

4.11 🎧

Root ends with:	Example	+ ed	<ed> sound	IPA
voiceless sound	stop	stop**ped**	/t/	/stɒpt/
	crack	crack**ed**		/krækt/
	mi**ss**	miss**ed**		/mɪst/
	lau**gh**	laugh**ed**		/lɑːft/
	ma**tch**	match**ed**		/mætʃt/
voiced sound	sta**r**	star**red**	/d/	/stɑːd/
	ru**b**	rub**bed**		/rʌbd/
	mu**g**	mug**ged**		/mʌgd/
	amu**se**	amus**ed**		/əmjuːzd/
	gath**er**	gather**ed**		/gæðəd/
/t/ or /d/	wan**t**	want**ed**	/ɪd/	/wɒntɪd/
	invi**te**	invit**ed**		/ɪnvaɪtɪd/
	pos**t**	post**ed**		/pəʊstɪd/
	roun**d**	round**ed**		/raʊndɪd/
	inva**de**	invad**ed**		/ɪnveɪdɪd/

45

EXERCISE

- Next to each word, write /t/, /d/ or /ɪd/ for the pronunciation of the < ed > ending:

stated _ɪd_ looked _t_ argued _d_ dubbed ___

capped ___ interested ___ deleted ___ sipped ___

sacked ___ annoyed ___ chewed ___ rated ___

shifted ___ retired ___ faced ___ blinded ___

flashed ___ loved ___ ended ___ pushed ___

decided ___ climbed ___ headed ___ inched ___

surfed ___ pulled ___ answered ___ intruded ___

2 🎧 - Listen and check your answers.

EXERCISE

- In each line of words, circle the odd one out:

A marked wished mixed killed kissed

B entered rated murdered ordered formed

C addressed designed judged lived opened

D closed missed fixed crossed expressed

E ended flooded needed twisted deepened

F claimed admired pleased joked flowed

4.13 🎧 - Listen to check your answers.

46

3 Syllable Words | Structure

- Listen to the words below. Where is the main stress in each?

4.14

manager   banana   entertain

- 3 syllable words can have the **main stress on the 1st, 2nd or 3rd syllables.**
- If the main stress is on the 3rd syllable, there will also be **secondary stress** on the 1st syllable.
- Secondary stress is marked / ˌ /. **EXAMPLE:** /ˌenterˈtain/

DRILL

- Repeat the rhythms and words in the chart below:

4.15

	Rhythm	Examples
1	X . . | X . . | X . . | X . .	brilliant, qualify, negative, wonderful, character
2	. X . | . X . | . X . | . X .	together, beginning, completion, collision, emotion
3	x . X | x . X | x . X | x . X	understand, disbelief, referee, magazine

---

EXERCISE

4.16

- Listen & circle the word in each line that contains a different stress pattern.

1. ignorant motivate nobody (politely) animal
2. inviting prevention relative eraser persuasion
3. passionate magazine Cantonese auctioneer afternoon
4. reflection impressive malicious interested invested
5. Africa Portugal Italy Jamaica Paraguay
6. professor lecturer musician translator consultant

EXERCISE

- Either by using a dictionary or the recording, place the words in the box into the correct column below:

> politics kangaroo supporter afternoon happily Portuguese believer satisfied Japanese courageous underneath clarify credible prevention quality seventeen tomorrow cigarette octopus energy annoying picturesque amusement funeral adventure serviette recommend reaction ignorant wonderful abolish refugee volunteer syllable consider

(X . .) 1st Syllable Stress	(. X .) 2nd Syllable Stress	(x . X) 3rd Syllable Stress
ˈpolitics	suˈpporter	ˌkangaˈroo

- Practise the words using the recording.

48

Yes/No Questions | Intonation

- Listen to the two conversations below:

4.18 🎧

A Have you seen the time?
B No, are we late?
A Yes₁ Don't you have a watch?
B No, but I have a phone. Could you pass it to me?

A Hello madam, Inspector Hoams. May I ask you some questions?
B Yes, go ahead.
A Were you at home last night?
B Yes, why? Has something happened?

- Underline the questions in the conversations.
- Which questions could be answered with 'yes' or 'no'?
- Is the intonation the same in every question?

- Yes/No questions normally use **rising** or **fall-rising** intonation.
- **Falling intonation** in a yes/no question sounds serious, formal or concerned.

DRILL

- Repeat the five questions below in three ways as follows:

4.19 🎧   a) Rising Intonation ↗

4.20 🎧   b) Fall-rising Intonation ↘↗

4.21 🎧   c) Falling Intonation ↘

- The tonic syllable in each question is in bold.

1. Does anybody have a **pen**?
2. Didn't you go **out** last night?
3. Can I ask you a **question**?
4. Will there be anyone I **know** there?
5. Were my **glasses** on the table?

EXERCISE

- Listen to each question twice and circle the intonation pattern you hear:

1. Does anybody have a **pen**? ↗ | ↘↗
2. Didn't you go **out** last night? ↘↗ | ↘
3. Can I ask you a **question**? ↘↗ | ↘
4. Will there be anyone I **know** there? ↘↗ | ↘
5. Were my **glasses** on the table? ↗ | ↘
6. Has anybody got a **camera**? ↗ | ↘
7. Are you coming to the **match**? ↗ | ↘↗
8. Would they like some more **tea**? ↘↗ | ↘

EXERCISE

- Listen to the conversations and practise saying them with the recording.

1.
A Are you coming out?
B No, I've got to wash my hair. Are you going anywhere nice?
A We're going to the pub. Can't you wash your hair tomorrow?
B Oh ok then. Can you give me 5 minutes to get ready?

2.
A Oh hello. May I speak to Mr. Smith?
B Yes. Could I ask who's calling?
A Yes, It's Mrs Jones.
B Mrs Jones, would you kindly tell me the reason for your call?
A I'm afraid it's personal. Is Mr Smith there? Or shall I call back?
B I will put you through, hold on.

3.
A Do you know this man?
A Have you ever seen him before?
A Did you have dinner with him last night?
A Will you please answer me?

Silent Syllables | Postscript

- Complete the crossword using the clues below.

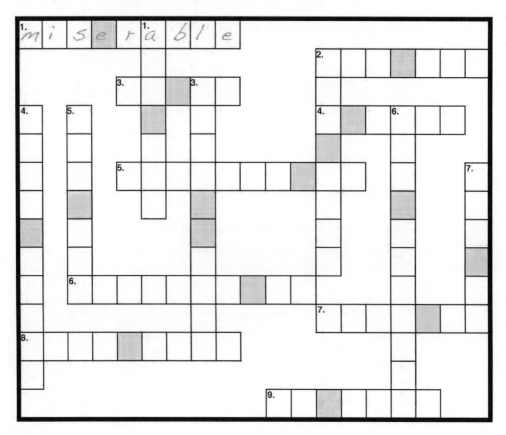

ACROSS

1. Very unhappy.
2. An unspecified number, more than two.
3. Drama set to music on stage.
4. Force devoted to crime prevention.
5. Book that lists words and their meanings.
6. A place used for scientific experimentation.
7. Everything that has happened in the past.
8. A sweet food made from cacao.
9. The most normal or middle value.

DOWN

1. A painkiller commonly used for headache.
2. Not together.
3. A place that serves food.
4. A formal meeting on a large scale.
5. Natural substance.
6. Not boring.
7. Those who are related by blood or marriage.

4.24   - Check your answers using the recording.
    - What is special about the grey squares?
    - Practise saying the words with the recording.

Chapter 5

Sounds	Short Vowels	ɪ ʊ e ʌ æ ɒ
Sound & Structure	/h/ Function h	
Spelling & Sound	Silent Letters	
Structure	Joining	
Intonation	Prominence	
Postscript	Verb / Noun	
		Answer Key Pages 121-122

Short Vowels | Sounds

- Listen to the sentence below. Is any vowel sound repeated?

5.1 🎧   "Jim's good friend's duck ran off!"

+ Spoken English contains **6 short vowel sounds:**					

Sound	Spellings	Examples	Mouth Position		
			Tongue	Lips	Jaw
I	i	pin, pick, bid, drink	mid front	relaxed	mid close
ʊ	u oo ou	push, bull, full, put cook, stood, good could, would, should	mid back	rounded	mid close
e	e ea/ie	pet, chef, slept, fresh bread, measure, friend	front	spread	mid
ʌ	u o ou	bus, duck, brush, fun none, money, done enough, rough	mid back	relaxed	mid open
æ	a	pat, sad, thank, pan	front	spread	open
ɒ	o a (q)ua	pot, sock, chop, gone what, want qualify, quantity	back	rounded	open

5.2 🎧

EXERCISE

- Place the words in the box below into the correct columns in the chart:

pull trust cash kick dog test could company bag quick fashion watch fence grill bush thorough value pleasure shift ready shop wrong mother ran look send hunt chip add wander bug wood butcher problem leisure wrist

ɪ	ʊ	e	ʌ	æ	ɒ

3 🎧 - Listen and check your answers.

DRILL

4 🎧

ɪ

This is history, listen! In sixteen sixty six, Britain didn't exist.

Tim's fitter than Jim, but Jim's thinner than him.

ʊ

I took the book to have a look.

The crook took the rook and put it on the bookshelf

e

Wendy sent Fred a red leather bed as a wedding present.

I bet ten cents on the reds.

ʌ

My son's in London having fun in the sun.

Money is not enough, nor blood, nothing comes close to love.

æ

The anarchist cat sat on the mat, having a chat with a radical rat.

In fact, the Titanic sank in the Atlantic.

ɒ

What do you want Tom? A vodka and tonic on the rocks? Or a strong coffee?

I want you to stop blocking my shop with boxes of rotten socks.

5.5 🎧
- Imagine you are steaming up a mirror.
- What sound do you produce?
- Where does this sound come from?

> ✦ English contains one **glottal fricative** sound /h/.
> ✦ /h/ only ever appears at the **beginning of a syllable**.

5.6 🎧

Sound	Spellings / Examples	Position
	< h, wh >	glottal
h	heat, whose, heard, hall, hard, hit, hood, ahead, hundred, hockey, hot, happy, behind, hope, hair.	

DRILL

5.7 🎧

h

How happy Harry was having seen Henry's house!
I hope Holland's hippies have hot holidays in Haiti.

< h > in Function Words | Structure

- Listen to the pronunciation of the word 'he' in this conversation:

    A "What's **he** doing?"

    B "**He**'s having lunch I think."

- How is the pronunciation different in the second line?

- The following function words begin with < h >:

    he, her, him, have, had, has, his.

- The < h > in these function words **is pronounced** if the function word is at the **beginning** or **end** of the sentence or phrase.
- This < h > will **normally be silent** in other positions of the sentence.
- Note that 'have', 'had' & 'has' also appear as content words (see pg 75).

EXERCISE

- Following the rules above, cross out the silent < h > and underline the pronounced < h > in the following sentences:

1. A Where's he gone?
B He said he was going to the bar.

2. A What does her brother do?
B Her brother? He's a plumber.

3. A How am I going to break the news to him?
B Sit him down, give him a cup of tea and explain slowly.

4. A Have we got a map in here?
B Oh no, we must have left it at home.

5. A What's his name?
B His first name's David, but I've forgotten his surname.

- Check your answers and practise the dialogues.

Silent Letters | Spelling & Sound

- Write the word for each picture in the gaps below them - each word contains a silent consonant:

5.10 🎧

_____ _____ _____ _____

> + Written English contains **consonant spellings that are never pronounced**.
> + Consonants < **b, h, k, l, n, p, s, t** & **w** > can be silent in speech.

DRILL

5.11 🎧

Silent Letter	Examples
b	debt, doubt, subtle, lamb, climb, numb, plumber, comb, thumb
h	honour, heir, hour, exhibit, exhaust, Thames
k	knee, know, knot, knife, knight
l	walk, talk, although, calf, half, chalk, yolk, calm, palm, salmon
n	column, autumn, condemn, damn, hymn
p	psychology, pneumonia, cupboard, receipt, pseudo, Psalm
s	island, aisle, debris
t	often, fasten, soften, listen, gourmet, mortgage, ballet
w	whole, who, sword, write, wrist, answer

EXERCISE

- Using the clues at the bottom of the page, fill in the crossword below. The grey letter in the middle contains a silent letter in each case.

```
1.              w
2.              b
3.              d
     4.         h
5.              g
     6.         t
          7.    k
     8.         l
          9.    w
  10.           g
  11.           w
12.             t
```

CLUES

1. The response to a question.
2. An inability to speak.
3. A woman's accessory, worn on the shoulder and where day-to-day things are kept.
4. The form of a dead person in an apparition.
5. Adjective. Originating from a different country or place.
6. The act of hearing something intently.
7. Verb. To use wool to create a garment using needles.
8. The yellow part of an egg.
9. Incorrect, the opposite of right.
10. An object or beahaviour indicating information.
11. The first light before sunrise in the morning.
12. The worker who delivers mail.

Joining Introduction | Structure

- Listen carefully to the sentence below.

5.12 🎧   **"Didn't_you_offer_Anne_Ball_lunch?"**

- How are the words joined where you see _ between words?

5.13 🎧
◆ In spoken English we aim to join words together to create smooth speech.
◆ There are different ways words and sounds can join as follows:

1. **consonant + consonant** joining

When 2 identical sounds appear next to eachother, we make one longer sound:

> Ball_lunch.
> I wish_Sharon well.

2. **consonant + consonant** assimilation

Some consonant sounds can join together to form a different sound (assimilate).
Most commonly this happens to /t/, /d/ & /n/:

didn't_you	t + j = tʃ
Anne_Ball	n + b = m
That_man	t + m = p

3. **consonant + vowel** joining

Final consonants move to the next syllable if the next syllable starts with a vowel:

> It _ isn't _ always _ easy. = /ɪ tɪ zən tɔ: weɪ zi: zi/
> Dan _ and _ Anne _ aren't _ in. = /dæ nə næ nɑ:n tɪn/

4. **vowel + vowel** joining

If one word ends with a vowel and the next begins with a vowel, we often join the words with one of /j/ /w/ or /r/:

you_offer	(you **w** offer)
We _ entered	(we **j** entered)
China _ expanded	(china **r** expanded)

EXERCISE

i) Write a line between all words that will have a consonant + vowel join:

1. What_a lot_of nonsense
2. It isn't at all bad
3. Can I take an apple?
4. I fell in love on holiday.
5. Her bank account is in the red.
6. It's a bit of a joke

ii) Repeat this recipe ensuring that the words are joined:

ITALIAN RECIPE
Wash and peel a tomato
Chop an onion
Heat a spoon of oil in a pan
Slice a bulb of garlic
Boil a pint of water with a pinch of salt
Cook a pound of pasta
Drain in a colander
Serve in a large bowl with olive oil.

iii) Circle the phrase in each line that will **assimilate**:

	word	Phrase 1	Phrase 2
1	hand	a handbag	hand it over!
2	bat	a bat and ball	Batman
3	grand	a grand party	a grand exit
4	London	London Underground	London Buses
5	down	down under	down below
6	red	a red car	a red apple
7	one	one metre	one inch

Prominence | Intonation

- Listen to the conversation:

5.17 🎧

A "Do you like pizza?"
B "I like all Italian food."

- Which words are stressed? Why?

> + In spoken English we give prominence (stress) to **new information**.
> + The **last word** with new information will be the strongest (tonic syllable).
> + We do not stress old information - "Italian food" in the example.

DRILL

- Listen and practise the conversations below, the prominent words are in **bold.**

5.18 🎧

A Would you like a **cup** of **tea**?
B I'm so **thirsty** I could drink a **pot** of tea!

A **Mozart's greatest work** was the St. **Matthew Passion**.
B That was **Bach's** work.

A Have you seen **Brad Pitt's latest**?
B **No**, I can't **stand** Brad Pitt!

A Do you **fancy going** to **Poland** this year?
B I wouldn't **mind** visiting **Cracow**.

A Has the **match finished**?
B **No**, the **first half** has finished.

A Would you like to **come** to **Warsaw** with me?
B **Absolutely**, I've **never been** to Poland before.

EXERCISE

- Reply to the recording using the sentence you are given.
- Underline the most important word in your reply (the last important word).

EXAMPLE 1.

"Can I get you anything to drink?"

Yes please, a cup of <u>tea</u>.

EXAMPLE 2.

"Was Betty Smith at the meeting"

No, but her husband <u>John</u> Smith was.

1. I'm scared of dogs.

2. Have you got anything by Kate Bush?

3. No, at three 'o' clock.

4. Well, you can't go wrong with a Mercedes.

5. It's a quarter to four.

6. I wouldn't mind a glass of white wine.

7. I think we should go to Spain.

8. No, I never listen to pop music.

9. I think it will be chicken and chips.

10. I'm not allowed sweet things.

- Turn your book upside down and practise the other part of each conversation:

PERSON A / RECORDING

1. Why don't you take Spot the dog for a walk?
2. What shall we listen to?
3. The game starts at four 'o' clock.
4. What car shall I buy?
5. What time is it?
6. Can I offer you some red wine?
7. Where shall we go on holiday?
8. Have you heard Kate Bush's new album?
9. What are you going to cook me for dinner?
10. Do you fancy an ice-cream?

Verb/Noun Stress Shift | Postscript

5.20 🎧

- Listen to the following dialogue, paying attention to the word 'refund':

   "I'd like a refund for these trousers – they don't fit."
   "I'm afraid we don't refund items over 28 days old sir."

- How does the stress change in 'refund'.

+ Some words' stress changes when the word changes from verb to noun.
+ As nouns, these words will use first syllable stress.
+ As verbs, they will use second syllable stress.

DRILL / EXERCISE

i) Repeat the words in the box, firstly as nouns then as verbs:

5.21 🎧

> conduct import export incense permit research progress
> object decrease contrast refund contract record present

ii) Use one word from the box for each pair of sentences below, marking the stress with < ' >:

1.
a) Is there any known _'research_ on the frequency of the schwa?
b) I have to _re'search_ Amazonian birds for my new book.

2.
a) The people of West Sussex _____ to the new power station.
b) The _____ of this exercise is to understand verb/noun pairs.

3.
a) Portugal will need to beat Poland to _____ in the competition.
b) _____ has been slow due to the terrible weather.

4.
a) "Excuse me sir, may I see your resident's _____."
b) We can't _____ you to bring this across the border.

5.
a) Recent years have seen a large _____ in crime.
b) If we _____ expenditure, I think profits will go up.

6.
a) I don't want any more nonsense, just _____ me with the facts.
b) Happy birthday Jane! Here's your _____.

5.22 🎧

- Listen and check your answers then practise the sentences.

Chapter 6

Sounds	Approximant Consonants	r j w l ł
Sound Comparison	Weak Vowels ɪ vs ə vs i	
Spelling & Sound	⟨ oo ⟩	
Structure	Vowel Joining	
Intonation	Question Tags	
Postscript	have'	

Answer Key Pages 123-124

Approximant Consonants | Sounds

> + An approximant is a **vowel-like consonant**.
> + The flow of air is **never fully blocked** in the production of approximants.
> + English contains three approximant sounds.

Sound	Spellings / Examples	Position
r 6.1	< r > read roof rich rub rock round rear prune pray true tree cry crash three through strong strike	alveolar
j	< j, u, i > yeast use youth usual yawn yard yes young yoghurt piano year tune tube	palatal
w	< w, u > weed word walk win wash wait always weird queen quick quote quiet conquest quarter	velar + rounded lips

DRILL

6.2

r
Great Britain's residents very rarely take breaks in Greenland.
Every Friday at three we rush to the bakery for fresh rye bread for breakfast.

j
I used to yearn to play a tune on your piano.
Yes, Janis, I ironed your yellow tunic yesterday, as usual.

w
Why not unwind with a quick weekend getaway in Wales.
Waiter, white wine for my wife, please and a whisky for me.

Lateral Approximants | Sounds

+ Lateral approximants are created by releasing air **past the sides of the tongue**.
+ < l > **before a vowel sound** will be pronounced /l/ with the tongue tip touching the alveolar ridge. This is sometimes called 'clear l'.
+ < l > **after a vowel sound** will be pronounced /ɫ/ with the tongue also raised at the back of the mouth. This is sometimes called 'dark l'.

sound	spellings / words	position
	< l >	alveolar
l	least lose learn left lock lazy life allow fly clip plot black bleed	
	< l >	alveolar (with tongue raised towards velum)
ɫ	real cool girl fall ball chill full melt fault rail boil style sold fold towel	

DRILL

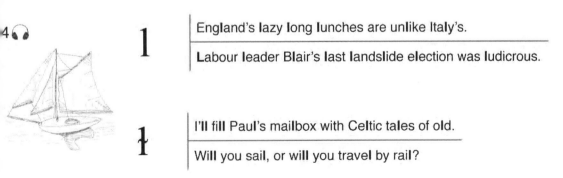

l	England's lazy long lunches are unlike Italy's.
	Labour leader Blair's last landslide election was ludicrous.
ɫ	I'll fill Paul's mailbox with Celtic tales of old.
	Will you sail, or will you travel by rail?

Weak ə vs ɪ | Sound Comparison

6.5 🎧
- Listen to four words with weak ending spelt < en >.
- Which word **does not** contain the schwa sound /ə/?

beat<u>en</u>   chick<u>en</u>   driv<u>en</u>   childr<u>en</u>

> + The **most common weak vowels of English** are /ə/ and /ɪ/.
> + These weak sounds are **spelt using < a, e, i, o & u >** in written English.
> + Weak vowels can appear at the beginning, middle and end of words.

DRILL

6.6 🎧   1. Words with /ə/:   mo<u>th</u>er tigh<u>ten</u> <u>pe</u>rform leg<u>al</u> <u>a</u>live dev<u>il</u> c<u>o</u>rrupt

2. Words with /ɪ/:   <u>e</u>nough wom<u>en</u> b<u>e</u>cause cott<u>age</u> fin<u>ish</u> tim<u>id</u>

EXERCISE

- Using a dictionary or the recording, place the words in the box into their correct column below. The weak form in each word is <u>underlined</u>.

accent erase kitchen fossil Thom<u>a</u>s <u>e</u>xplain man<u>age</u> evil China or<u>ange</u>
purch<u>ase</u> kiss<u>es</u> madn<u>ess</u> p<u>e</u>rsuade counc<u>il</u> r<u>e</u>turn band<u>age</u> harvest Japan
d<u>e</u>mand dang<u>er</u> English miss<u>es</u> gard<u>en</u> lent<u>il</u> b<u>e</u>lieve Engl<u>and</u> p<u>a</u>rade wick<u>ed</u>
defence turning spoken pencil surface

ə	ɪ
accent	*erase*

6.7 🎧   - Check your answers and practise saying the words.

67

Weak i vs ɪ | Sound Comparison

- Listen carefully to the following sentence:

3 🎧   "France's tax**i**s don't pay tax**e**s!"

- Can you hear a difference in the pronunciation of 'taxis' and 'taxes'?

Weak /i/

6.9 🎧   ✦ The long vowel /iː/ also appears in spoken English as a **short, weak vowel** /i/.
     ✦ It appears at the end of words spelt < y >, and in pronouns ending < e >:

Content Words		Function Words	
finally	/faɪnəli/	me	/mi/
only	/əʊnli/	she	/ʃi/
early	/ɜːli/	we	/wi/

Weak /ɪ/

.10 🎧   ✦ The short vowel /ɪ/ also appears in spoken English as a weak form.
     ✦ As a weak vowel it **never appears at the end of a syllable**.
     ✦ In function words it is always spelt < i >.

Content Words		Function Words	
wanted	/wɒntɪd/	him	/hɪm/
incredible	/ɪnˈkredɪbəl/	with	/wɪð/
managing	/mænɪdʒɪŋ/	this	/ðɪs/

EXERCISE

- In the sentences below, write ɪ or i above each weak vowel underlined in **bold**:

🎧

1. What does h**e** want w**i**th th**i**s carp**e**t?

2. I'm meet**i**ng Mand**y** th**i**s even**i**ng.

3. Sh**e**'s vis**i**t**i**ng from Burnl**ey**.

4. D**i**d w**e** reall**y** need to fin**i**sh the whisk**ey**?

5. If Kat**y** **i**s w**i**th m**e**, w**e**'ll eat sush**i**.

6. Johnn**y** nearl**y** crashed into m**e**.

7. D**i**d h**e** reall**y**? How **i**nconsiderate of h**i**m!

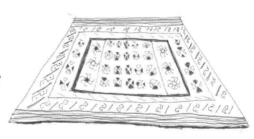

< oo > | Spelling & Sound

- Listen to the sentence below:

6.12 🎧   **"Lo**ok at the **flo**od on the **poo**r m**oo**n."

- How many different vowel sounds appear in the < oo > spelling?

> • The spelling < oo > is most commonly pronounced /u:/.
> • Some words spelt with < oo > are pronounced /ʊ/ or /ʌ/
> • The spelling < oor > is pronounced /ɔ:/
> • The word 'brooch' is pronounced /brəʊtʃ/

EXERCISE

- Listen to the words in the box and place them into the correct column of the table below:

6.13 🎧

troop stood wood fool book blood food soon shook took moor wool brook cook cool flood foot poor roof good smooth floor zoom balloon look shampoo door rook zoo hood tooth hook room

1	2	3	4
< oo > = /ʊ/	< oo > = /u:/	< oo > = /ʌ/	< oo > = /ɔ:/
stood	troop		

-

69

EXERCISE

- Navigate from start to finish *without* saying the sound /uː/.
- You may move vertically or horizontally, **NOT diagonally**.

START

groom	cook	roof	pool	root	school
good	foot	soon	loose	zoom	boot
hood	room	door	flood	look	food
wool	blood	stood	zoo	took	bloom
tooth	moon	mood	shoot	shook	scoop
balloon	proof	boom	fool	woof	tool
choose	shampoo	mushroom	goose	floor	too

FINISH

Vowel + Vowel Joining | Structure

- Listen to the 2 word phrases - how do they join together?

6.14

Lisa Adams.

Free us!

Go out!

+ When one word ends with a vowel sound and the next word begins with a vowel sound, **we will normally join** the words in speech.
+ In order to join, we will add an approximant sound: /r/ /j/ or /w/.
+ The **joining approximant is often shown in the spelling** of the first word.

1. Joining with /w/

6.15 + If the first word ends in a rounded vowel (u, əʊ, aʊ), we join with /w/.

who_are you   go_away   now_and then

2. Joining with /j/

+ If the first word ends in a high vowel (i, eɪ, aɪ, ɔɪ) we join with /j/.

we_understand   pay_up   try_it

3. Joining with /r/

+ If the first word ends in a neutral vowel (ə, ɜ:, ɔ:, eə, ɪə) we join with /r/.

brother_and sister   war_and peace   law_and order.

+ Words spelt with <aw> such as 'law', 'saw' etc. join with /r/.

DRILL

This voice exercise is designed to move the mouth for vowel + vowel joining:

6.16
1. Joining with /w/   uːwə əʊwə aʊwə
2. Joining with /j/   iːjə eɪjə ɔɪjə aɪjə
3. Joining with /r/   ɜːrə ɔːrə ɑːrə ɪərə eərə

71

EXERCISE

- Place the sentences into their correct columns according to the joiner:

Can you see_it?   Can you hear_it?   Joe_isn't here.

I'll bring your tray_up in a minute.   Fry_it in a little oil.

They're mother_and daughter. The two_of you will win!

Are we near_Oxford?   That's so_exciting!

The day_after tomorrow.   No sir_I can't help.

Can we buy_a new toaster?   How_about a tea?

It's the law_of averages.   A toy_elephant.   You'll get through_it.

Who_are you?   I feel free_as a bird   Now_and then

Can you spare_a minute?

j	w	r
Can you see it?	Joe isn't here.	Can you hear it?

 - Listen and check your answers.

DRILL

- Say the following names joining the first name with the surname each time:

 Joe Adams   Roy Edwards   Lisa Ashford   Sue Ingrids   Joy Austin
Claire Anthony   Teresa Elmsfield   Charlie Edwards   Emma Ellis

Question Tags | Intonation

- Listen to the following statement said in two ways:

6.19 🎧

"Hello, you're Katie, aren't you?"

- How is the meaning different each time?

> ✦ A question tag is added to a statement to make it into a question.
> ✦ Most question tags are opposite to their statement (negative/positive or positive/negative) and use the following intonation:
>   - **Falling intonation**, meaning "I know what I am saying is correct".
>   - **Rising intonation**, meaning "I am not sure, please answer".
> ✦ Question tags are very common in British English but rare in American English.

DRILL

1. Say the following statement and tag combinations with **falling intonation**:

6.20 🎧

That's a beautiful piece of art, ↘isn't it?
They were so noisy, ↘weren't they?
Susan will be on her way by now, ↘won't she?
He can run really fast, ↘can't he?
This film will win awards, ↘won't it?
Arsenal are brilliant, ↘aren't they?

2. Say the following statement and tag combinations with **rising intonation**:

6.21 🎧

John's finished his exams, ↗hasn't he?
It's not ten 'o' clock yet, ↗is it?
The Smiths were at the party, ↗weren't they?
That's your car, ↗isn't it?
John can't play the trumpet, ↗can he?
You don't think England will win, ↗do you?

EXERCISE

- Listen to the conversation:

2 🎧

A You won't forget to call me when you arrive in New York, [1]↘will you?

B I'll try not to mum.

A And you know that the subway is dangerous at night, [2]↘don't you?

B Yes mum.

A And if anyone strange approaches you, you'll walk away, [3]↘won't you?

B You think I'm stupid, [4]↘don't you? I can look after myself you know?

A Yes darling, but you can't be too careful these days, [5]↘can you?
And you're my son, so I'm allowed to worry....... [6]↗aren't I?

B Yes mum, of course you are.

- Why does the mother use falling intonation in tags 1 - 5?
- In tag 6 the mother uses rising intonation. Why?

EXERCISE

- Listen to the conversation then practise saying it.

3 🎧

A Excuse me, you aren't Billy ↗are you?

B Yes, who's asking?

A You don't recognise me, ↘do you?

B Well, I'm not sure. You seem familiar.

A I can't believe it. But you remember going to college in Oxford, ↗don't you?

B How could I forget?

A And you haven't forgotten the drama club, ↗have you?

B No, of course not. Ahh Liz, Liz Jones. It's ten years since we saw each other last, ↗isn't it?

A Yes, it must be. Well, how are you?

- Explain the use of intonation in each tag.

74

'have' | Postscript

- Listen to the dialogue:

6.24 🎧

A What **have** you got planned for this evening?

B I **have** to work on my thesis.

A That's a shame. We're going to **have** sushi in the centre.

B **Have** you tried sushi before?

A No, but the others **have**. Have you?

B I might **have** done once, ages ago.

A Well, we'll **have** to go out another night.

B Absolutely, **have** fun!

- How many different ways is the word 'have' pronounced?

6.25 🎧 ◆ The pronunciation of 'have' **changes depending on its usage** as follows:

Usage	Pronunciation	Examples
content	/hæv/	I have red hair.
stressed function		I *have* finished.
function word	/həv/	Have the police arrived?
	/əv/	What have you done?
	/v/	I've finished the biscuits.
modal obligation	/hæf/	We have to go now.

EXERCISE

- Go through the conversation at the top of the page and find an example of each pronunciation of 'have' from the table.
- Create your own examples for each usage of 'have'.

75

Chapter 7

Sounds	Diphthong Vowels	eɪ ɔɪ aɪ əʊ aʊ ɪə eə
Spelling & Sound	⟨ o ⟩	
Structure	Compounds	
Intonation	High Fall	
Postscript	'do'	
	Answer Key Pages 125-126	

Diphthong Vowels | Sounds

7.1 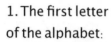   - What sound do English people say for the following:

1. The first letter
of the alphabet:

2. To grab someone's
attention:

3. What we use to see with:

5. The invisible substance we
breathe:

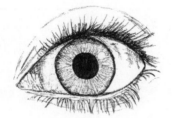

4. What we say when
we are hurt:

6. What we use to hear with:

7. What we say when we are surprised:

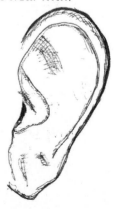

+ A diphthong is a long vowel that moves from **one mouth position to another**.
+ The **first position** in a diphthong is **stronger than the second**:

Sound	Spellings	Examples	Position 1 tongue I jaw	Position 2 tongue I jaw
eɪ	ay, ea, a_e, ai	pay, break, grade, fail, stay, wait, change	front | mid	front | close
ɔɪ	oi, oy	boy, toy, avoid, foil, enjoy, annoy, coin	back | mid	front | close
aɪ	ie, i_e, i, y	pie, crime, climb, spy, shine, fly, high	back | open	front | close
əʊ	o, o_e, oa, ow	post, tone, soap, show, so, lonely, soda	flat | mid	back | close
aʊ	ou, ow	couch, house, allow, brown, voucher, noun, how	front | open	back | close
ɪə	eer, ear	peer, gear, steer, fear, beer, rear, cheer, spear	front | close	flat | mid
eə	are, ere, ea, ai	spare, where, pair, care, there, aware dare	front | mid	flat | mid

DRILL

eɪ

The rain in Spain never came, what a shame

Pay the waiter to take the tray away.

ɔɪ

Roy annoyed his boy by toying with some foil.

The Royals employed Mrs. Doyle to boil their soil.

aɪ

Di tried to ride her bike from Brighton to the Isle of Skye.

Bide your time Mr. Vine, but sign under the right line.

əʊ

Go, don't moan, and phone me when you get home.

Joe wrote an emotional post-it note.

aʊ

How now brown mouse?

Around this town they found some astounding grounds.

ɪə

Near here, you can clearly hear the deer.

Sorry Shakespeare, King Lear was clearly really weird

eə

The heir to the mayor, let's hope he's fair, Mr. Blair!

Rare bear's hairs are carefully aired in there.

Diphthongs | Sound Comparison

EXERCISE

- Complete the blank squares with words only using the consonant on the left + the diphthong on the top, then check your answers and listen to the words.

	eɪ	ɔɪ	aɪ	əʊ	aʊ	ɪə	eə
b	bay	boy	buy				
d							
m							
p							
r							
s							
t							
w							

EXERCISE

- Complete the IPA transcription for the pictures. **Use each diphthong only once.**

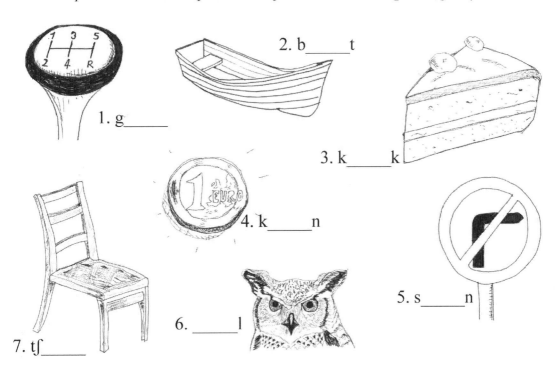

1. g_____

2. b_____t

3. k_____k

4. k_____n

5. s_____n

6. _____l

7. tʃ_____

80

< o > | Spelling & Sound

- Listen to the sentence below:

7.5 🎧 "Wh**o**'s st**o**len my s**o**n's b**o**xing g**o**wn?"

- Which vowel sounds appear on each <o>?

> • The spelling < o > commonly produces /əʊ/ /ʌ/ /ɒ/ and /u:/ in pronunciation.
> • Exceptions are 'w**o**men' /wɪmɪn/, 'w**o**man' /wʊmən/ & 'w**o**lf' /wʊlf/
> • The spelling < ow > produces /əʊ/ & /aʊ/.
> • The spelling < or > usually produces /ɔ:/.

EXERCISE

- Listen to the words in the box and place them into the correct column of the table below:

7.6 🎧

month long move comb how down bold cod do tongue front log now alone cross shot cow lose so shove tomb allow cold prove some dock love who brown low

< o > = /ɒ/	< o > = /ʌ/	< o > = /əʊ/	< o > = /u:/	< o > = /aʊ/
long	month			

EXERCISE

- Using the directional arrows in the key below, go down the board.

KEY								
sound	əʊ	ɒ	ʌ	ɔ:	ɪ	ʊ	u:	aʊ
direction	↓	↙	↘	↖	↑	↗	←	→

START

dose	gone	bowl	sock	nose	flow	fox
done	doll	wrong	bone	whole	wonder	hole
gown	owl	so	stole	brown	nothing	pony
phone	London	son	boss	women	drown	grown
chop	shower	none	wolf	one	stop	not
dog	rope	Rome	born	chop	do	lost
dock	show	port	lose	store	home	posh
town	love	come	chose	rot	other	who

FINISH   **FINISH**   **FINISH**   **FINISH**   **FINISH**   **FINISH**   **FINISH**

- Where do you exit at the bottom? Check your answer and route in the answer key.

Compounds | Structure

- Listen to the following words, where is the main stress?

7.7 🎧   catfish deadline figurehead homesick lawsuit waterfall

> + A compound is **formed of two words**.
> + Compounds **can be written as** one word, two words separated by a hyphen, or two separate words.
> + Most compounds place **stress only on the first word**.

DRILL

7.8 🎧   airport background bedtime breakfast bulldog cobweb
          cupboard deadline doorway eyelash farmhouse fingernail
          gateway goldfish grandmother grapefruit hairdresser
          headphones hangover honeymoon windowsill left over
          motorbike popcorn seashore shellfish sometimes stepmother

EXERCISE

- In the conversation below, underline the compound nouns:

7.9 🎧   A Hello <u>granddad</u>!
          B Oh hello darling, how nice to receive a telephone call from you!
          A How are you and grandma?
          B Oh we're very well.
             We're just sitting here reading the newspapers.
          A Is there anything interesting?
          B No, not really. What's your news?
             Are you still with your boyfriend, Greg?
          A Actually, that's why I called.
             Yesterday Greg proposed!
             I'm wearing an engagement ring right now!
          B Well, congratulations darling.
             I always thought I could hear wedding bells with you two!

- Check your answers and practise saying the conversation.
- Which compounds are written as two separate words?

83

EXERCISE

- Name the household objects in the pictures. They are all compounds:

High Fall | Intonation

- Listen to the following typical exchange said in 2 ways:

7.11 🎧   A "It's a lovely day, isn't it?"

B "Yes, absolutely gorgeous"

- How did the meaning change the second time?

+ A falling pattern **can start from a high tone** (high-fall) or a **mid tone** (mid-fall).
+ The **meaning changes** radically when the different tones are used.
+ A high-fall shows **enthusiasm, emotion** and **involvement** in the speaker.
+ A mid-fall shows **detachment, lack of interest** and even **boredom**.
+ The high-fall is very **common in spoken English** - see drill below.

DRILL

7.12 🎧

STATEMENTS & NEW INFORMATION	'Paris is so charming in spring.' 'I'm really looking forward to my holiday'. 'Let's make a cake!'
INFORMATION QUESTIONS	'What's the weather like?' 'Who will be at your party?' 'How much are these trousers?'
QUESTION TAGS (STATEMENTS)	'It's great, isn't it?' 'Those children are so lively, aren't they?' 'Elena was a brilliant cook, wasn't she?
EXCLAMATIONS	'Wonderful!' 'Brilliant!' 'Fantastic!'

EXERCISE

i) Listen to the conversation:

A Hi Jane!

B Oh hi John! I haven't seen you for ages!

A No, it must be 2 years now.

B Yes, it was in London, wasn't it?

A Yes, at the old friends reunion. Anyway, how are things?

B Pretty good! I've been working on a new book.

A Oh yes. What's this one about?

B It's a biography of a 16th century scientist.

A Wow! How interesting! When will it be finished?

B Oh I hope very soon. And how have you been?

A You didn't hear, did you? Katie had a baby last year! A little boy.

B Amazing! You're a father!
   Congratulations. Who would have thought it?

A Yes, I can't quite believe it myself.

B What's his name?

A Peter. I preferred Jethro, but Kate insisted.

B Peter's a lovely name. Listen, I must be off! I have a train to catch.

A Fine, we must meet up soon!

B Absolutely. I'll give you a call.

ii) Every underlined sentence/unit uses a high-fall. Choose the usage from the list below for each high-fall:

- Information
- Exclamation
- Information Question
- Statement Question Tag

iii) Practise the conversation using a high-fall where indicated.

'do' | Postscript

- Listen to the dialogue:

7.14

A How do the English say a schwa sound?
B Don't you know yet?
A No, I don't. Where do you put the lips.
B You don't move the lips, they stay still.
A What do you do with the tongue?
B Well, you don't do anything with it, it's relaxed.
A Amazing, do you do anything with the jaw?
B No, absolutely not. To make a schwa, you do nothing.
A Why does it always come out wrong then?
B Maybe you're no good at doing nothing!

+ The verb 'do' has the following pronunciations in spoken English:

də   dəʊnt   duː   duːwɪŋ   dʒu

- Listen and write the pronunciation from the box above next to each usage below:

7.15
i) The negative form (don't) is pronounced _____.
ii) The weak function word (do) is pronounced _____.
iii) The stressed or content word (do) is pronounced _____.
iv) The gerund form (doing) is pronounced _____.
v) The weak function words 'do you' can be pronounced _____.

EXERCISE

- Write the expected pronunciation of 'do' next to each sentence:

7.16
1. Do they know we're coming? _____
2. Do you like my new haircut? _____
3. You do love me, don't you? _____ _____
4. If you do come, we'll have a great time. _____
5. Don't you fancy a night out? _____
6. Do we really need another car? _____
7. Phil's left me. What am I going to do? _____

- Listen to check your answers.

Chapter 8

Sounds	Nasal Consonants	m n ŋ
Sound Comparison	ŋ vs ŋg	△
Spelling & Sound	⟨ a ⟩	
Structure	Double Stress Compounds	
Intonation	Fall‿rise	
Postscript	are'	
		Answer Key Pages 127-128

Nasal Consonants | Sounds

> + A nasal consonant is a voiced sound made with air **escaping through the nose**.
> + There are three nasal consonants in spoken English.

Sound	Spellings / Examples	Position
8.1 🎧 **m**	< m > mean music mist mate might amazing lamb team came home drum	bilabial (both lips)
n	< n > need north next name near interfere enlist investigate land bone soon barn	alveolar
ŋ	< nk, ng > think twinkle sunk monk bank England thing song language working singing	velar

DRILL

8.2 🎧

m
Millions of **m**ad **m**issionaries **m**istook a **m**ember of parliament for the **m**afia.

Maybe so**m**ething will a**m**aze you in **m**y A**m**erican **m**ansion.

n
I **n**ever **n**oticed **N**elly turning **n**i**n**ety.

Do **n**ot complai**n** by telepho**n**e, i**n**stead se**n**d a **n**ote.

ŋ
Whilst walki**ng** I was si**ng**i**ng** a so**ng** about E**ng**land's mo**nk**s.

I'm hu**ng**ry so I'm goi**ng** to eat someth**ng**.

Nasal Assimilations | Sounds

- Say the sentence below as it is written:

3 🎧

Londom Bridge looks iŋcredible tonight!

3.4 🎧 ◆ In connected speech, the sound /n/ **often assimilates** to /m/ and /ŋ/.
◆ The assimilation can occur if the **following consonant is bilabial or velar**:

Assimilation	Example 1	Example 2
n + bilabial cons (p, b, m) = m	Ista**m**bul i**m**-**b**etween	i**m m**y tha**m P**eter
n + velar consonant (k, g) = ŋ	E**ŋg**land i**ŋc**rease	su**ŋ c**ream i**ŋ G**reece

EXERCISE

i) Listen to the names of 10 people & write the first name above its surname.

ii) In brackets next to each first name, write 'm', 'n', or 'ŋ' according to the pronunciation of < n >.

Anne   Ken   Aaron   John   Jane   Karen   Ben   Wayne   Sean   Lauren

5 🎧

First Name	*Anne (m)*				
Surname	Peters	Cole	Lane	Carter	Grove
First Name					
Surname	Bates	Edwards	Bailey	Thomas	Mayfield

iii) For every < n > in the sentences below, write either 'n' 'm' or 'ŋ' above to show its pronunciation then listen and check.

6 🎧

1. Have you bee**n** playi**ŋ** o**ŋ** Katie's computer agai**n**?

2. Win cars, win money and win big prizes tonight!

3. On paper the ban could work, but in reality it won't.

4. Can I have a thin piece of Belgian cake?

5. I'll telephone you when my son can come.

90

/ŋ/ vs /ŋg/ | Sound Comparison

- Listen carefully to the words below:

8.7

singer   single   finger

- Which word **does not** contain a /g/ sound?

EXERCISE

- Listen to the words in the box and put them into the correct columns below according to the pronunciation of < ng >.

8.8

taxing finger thing hunger England Hungary
sting working wing stronger longer bang mango
wrongly tango movingly singer single angle

ŋ	ŋg
taxing	finger

- From your answers, how is < ng > pronounced:

        (i) at the **end of a word**?
        (ii) in **superlatives** and **comparatives**?
        (iii) when it appears in the **middle** of a word?

/ŋ/

* < ng > is pronounced /ŋ/ without a following /g/ sound at the end of words.
    EXAMPLES: taxing, working, wing, bang

* If we add an ending to a word ending /ŋ/ it will not change *unless* it is a comparative or superlative.
    EXAMPLES: singer, wrongly, movingly

/ŋg/

* Words that contain < ng > followed by more letters *that have not been added as an ending* will be pronounced /ŋg/.
    EXAMPLES: hunger, England, Hungary, tango

* Adjectives ending < ng > made into superlatives or comparatives (-est/er) will be pronounced with /ŋg/.
    EXAMPLES: stronger, longer

EXERCISE

- Circle the odd word out in each line:

1. bang   banger   Bangladesh

2. hungry   hunger   hung

3. young   younger   youngest

4. angle   angry   along

5. England   English   speaking

6. hanger   finger   anger

7. triangle   angler   wrongly

8. Congo   bingo   ringing

9. slang   language   linguistics

10. stronger   strong   strongest

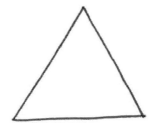

< a > | Spelling & Sound

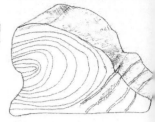

- Listen to the following sentence:

8.11 🎧   He wanted raw tuna, but Dave asked the waiter for rare village lamb.

- How many different vowel sounds are produced on the spelling <a>?

◆ The spelling < a > can produce **7 strong vowel sounds**:

Drill

8.12 🎧

Spelling	Sound	Examples
al	ɔː	ball, fall, call, walk, talk
	ɑː	calm, palm, half, calf
ar	ɑː	bar, far, hard, spark, sharp
aw	ɔː	yawn, paw, law, raw, saw
ay/ai	eɪ	pay, paid, day, stay, ray, laid
a_e	eɪ	range, made, Dave, rave, bathe
	eə	dare, stare, share, bare, flare
a	æ	hat, back, match, band
	ɑː	father, rather, ask, past, task
w(h)a	ɒ	what, watch, want, wand, wasn't, wash

◆ < a > can also produce **2 weak vowel sounds**:

a	ə	about, arrange, particular, parade, machine
-age	ɪ	manage, spillage, village, cottage

EXERCISE

- Write the word for each IPA transcription in the gap then find it in the crossword below.

wɒsp _wasp_

ætləs _____

seɪf _____

speə _____

ræp _____

ʃɑːk _____

hɑːf _____

wɒt _____

tʃeɪs _____

ɑːsk _____

sɔːlt _____

wɒtʃ _____

geɪt _____

hæt _____

tɔːk _____

ʃwaː _____

sɔː _____

wɒz _____

s	c	h	w	a	s
k	w	h	a	t	s
l	a	a	s	l	a
a	t	x	p	a	f
t	c	h	a	s	e
s	h	a	r	k	a
g	a	t	e	h	w

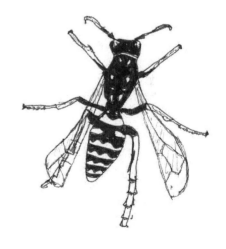

Name Compounds | Structure

- Listen to the following place names. Which one uses a different stress pattern?

8.13 🎧 Cambridge Road   Regent's Park   Oxford Street   Church Way

---

8.14 🎧 ◆ Names of **people and places** carry double stress (x X)

EXAMPLES: John Smith, Church Road, Blue Peter, Count Dracula

◆ The only exception to this rule are **names with 'Street'**, which always take first element stress. (X .)

EXAMPLES: Church Street, Wall Street, Beale Street, High Street.

EXERCISE

- Say the following names of places in London:
- Which names use first element stress?

8.15 🎧

Oxford Circus
Goodge Street
Hampstead Heath
London Bridge
Cannon Street
Covent Garden
Notting Hill
Hyde Park
Abbey Road
Bond Street
Kensington Gardens
Liverpool Street

EXERCISE

- Listen to 2 people introduce themselves with their names and addresses, write the information below:

8.16 🎧 1. NAME _____ _____ ADDRESS _____ _____
2. NAME _____ _____ ADDRESS _____ _____

- Say your name and address, paying attention to the stress in the compounds.

95

Material & Ingredient Compounds | Structure

- Listen to the dialogue and find 2 compounds:

A What's your favourite desert?
B Well I love pear tart, but probably my favourite is carrot cake.

- Are the compounds single or double stressed?

3.18 ♦ When a material or ingredient is the **first word of a compound**, it normally produces **double stress (x X)** as follows:

1st Word	2nd Word
cheese	sandwich
tuna	quiche
lettuce	salad
wooden	floor
metal	lock
leather	shoes

♦ 3 exceptions to this rule are when **the second word is 'cake', 'juice' or 'drink'**, these produce **first element stress (X .).**

1st Word	Second Word
orange	juice
carrot	cake
banana	drink

EXERCISE

- In each line of compounds, circle the odd one out:

1. apple juice   apple cake   (apple tart)   Apple Street
2. John Edwards   tin can   ham sandwich   potato cake
3. chocolate cake   mango juice   woolen jumper   chocolate drink
4. train ticket   lamp shade   glass cabinet   dining table
5. suede shoes   leather trousers   dinner jacket   cotton shirt
6. fruit juice   banana smoothie   filter coffee   coffee cake

Implicational Fall-rise | Intonation

- Listen to each dialogue said in two different ways.
- How does the meaning differ the second time?

8.20

A What was the film like?
B I enjoyed it.

A Would you like to go out tonight for dinner?
B Yes

A What do you think about Mary?
B She's very stylish.

- Using fall-rise intonation on a statement produces an **implication** - similar to saying "but".
- This use of the fall-rise is often used to **subtly criticise or show doubt**.
- A **falling pattern** on a statement gives it a **direct**, **non-implied** meaning.

DRILL

- Produce each sentence firstly using falling, then using fall-rising intonation:

8.21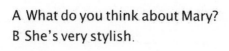

1. I'd **like** to go with you.
2. She's a good **teacher**.
3. It's very **expensive**.
4. I'm sure he **will**.
5. I think it's **good**

EXERCISE

- Decide if the underlined part of each conversation will use falling intonation for a direct meaning or fall-rising for implicational meaning:

1.

a)
A Look, if you don't want to go with me to Paris, just say so. ☐↘ ☐↘↗
B No, but listen, I'd **like** to go with you. Let's book it now!

b)
A Would you like to come to the dog hairstyle awards with me? ☐↘ ☐↘↗
B Well, I'd **like** to go with you, but I'm terribly busy at the moment.

2.

a)
A What do you think of Margaret? ☐↘ ☐↘↗
B Well, she's a good **teacher**, I'm not so sure about her dress sense.

b)
A I've learnt so much from Margaret this term. ☐↘ ☐↘↗
B I'm sure you have! She's a good **teacher**!

3.

a)
A What made you decide on a Gucci watch? ☐↘ ☐↘↗
B Well, it's very **expensive**, but the quality is worth it.

b)
A Why don't you want to buy the vase? ☐↘ ☐↘↗
B Because it's very **expensive**!

4.

a)
A Davey will enjoy this film, it stars Nicole Kidman. ☐↘ ☐↘↗
B Yes I'm sure he **will**!

b)
A Joe hasn't done his homework. ☐↘ ☐↘↗
B I know , but I'm sure he **will**.

5.

a)
A What do you think of the collection? ☐↘ ☐↘↗
B I think it's **good**, but it could be more varied.

b)
A Lots of people have criticized the policy. ☐↘ ☐↘↗
B Well, I think it's **good**. How about you?

2🎧 - Listen to check your answers then practise the conversations.

98

'are' | Postscript

- Listen to the conversation paying attention to the **bold** words:

8.23 🎧

"The Smiths **are** going to be at the party, **aren't** they?"
"What ***are*** you talking about? The Smiths **are** in Portugal!"

- How many different pronunciations did you hear of the word 'are'?

· The pronunciation of 'are' depends on its **stress**, **function** and **position**:

8.24 🎧 **Weak Form:** /ə/ (/ər/ if followed by a vowel)

What are you doing here?
Linda and Josh are visiting at the weekend!
Why are we even talking about this?
I think we're interested in the blue one.

Strong Form: /ɑː/ (/ɑːr/ if followed by a vowel)

Who are you?
So what if we are?
I don't know if we *are* happy together.
Oh dear, we *are* in trouble then.

Negative Form: /ɑːnt/

Why aren't you wearing a suit?
There aren't any biscuits left!
We aren't at all pleased.
But you're coming along, aren't you?

EXERCISE

- Write the pronunciation of 'are' into each gap using the transcriptions in the box:

> ə (x3) ər (x1) ɑːnt (x1) ɑː (x1)

8.25 🎧

The blues ___ attacking now, they ___ really pushing up the field.
Where ___ the red defenders. There ___ four blue attackers in the
box, they ___ waiting for the cross. Goal, and there ___ many as
glorious as that.

99

Chapter 9

Sounds	Affricate Consonants	tʃ dʒ
Sound Comparison	Long vs Short	
Spelling & Sound	Contractions	
Structure	Stress Shift	13 14 15
Intonation	Adverbials	
Postscript	Phrasal Verbs	
		Answer Key Pages 129-130

Affricate Consonants | Sounds

> ◆ An affricate consonant sound **starts as a plosive**, then **releases into a fricative**.
> ◆ There are two affricate consonants in spoken English.

Sound	Spelling / Examples	Position 1	Position 2
9.1 🎧 tʃ	< ch, tch > cheat charm chip check chop China cheer each watch catch rich bunch such	alveolar	postalveolar
dʒ	< j, g, dg > jeans June urge jaw jar gin fridge just judge jump rage age mortgage magician		

DRILL

9.2 🎧 **tʃ**

Chet and Charles are like chalk and cheese.

Such cheap Chilean chocolates made Butch wretch.

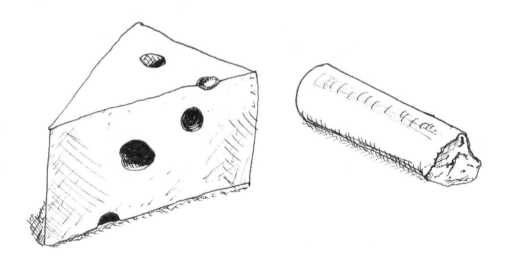

dʒ

Judge Geoffrey Jones genuinely enjoyed his gin.

Joe's small budget and large mortgage mean no jewels for Jane.

tʃ & dʒ Assimilations | Sounds

- Listen to the sentence below:

"Did you try the drinks on Tuesday?"

- How many affricates are pronounced?
- How are they spelt?
- In each case is there an alternative pronunciation?

• The following assimilations are very common in spoken English:

Assimilation		Example Word	Example Joining Words
t + j	tʃ	Tuesday (tʃuːzdeɪ or tjuːzdeɪ)	that you (ðætʃu or ðæt ju)
d + j	dʒ	due (dʒuː or djuː)	did you (dɪdʒu or dɪd ju)
t + r	tʃr	try (tʃraɪ or traɪ)	NOT POSSIBLE
d + r	dʒr	drain (dʒreɪn or dreɪn)	NOT POSSIBLE

✦The weak combination 'do you' is often contracted to /dʒu/ in speech.

EXERCISE

- There are **2 possible assimilations** to /tʃ/ and /dʒ/ in every line. Underline them:

1. Would you like to hear my tune?
2. When did your train arrive?
3. Draw a tree in the background.
4. The box had 'Europe' traced onto its lid.
5. Do you know how to drive?
6. Might your tulips flower this month?
7. The duke is coming for lunch this Tuesday.
8. There's a bit of a draft, could you close the window?
9. Aren't you coming to the studio?
10. I'm sorry, I just don't trust you.

- Listen to check your answers and practise the sentences.

Long vs Short Vowels | Sound Comparison

EXERCISE

i) Make words using the consonants and vowels in the box below (names of people and places are not allowed).

▓ = no word possible or uncommon word.

	æ	ɑː	ɒ	ɔː	e	ʌ	ɜː
b_t	bat	▓	▓	bought	bet	but	▓
p_t	pat	part	pot	port	pet	putt	pert
t_n		▓	▓				
h_t				▓	▓		
k_t					▓		
b_d			▓				
w_k		▓			▓		
b_n			▓		▓		

ii) Write the IPA transcription for the pictures below. They all appear in the chart above:

hæt

DRILL

- Without using the recording, create two words from each box.

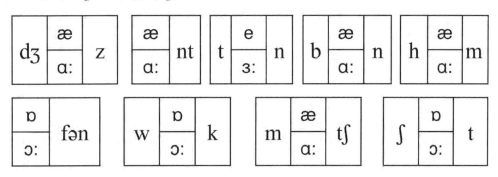

🎧 - Repeat the pairs of words with the recording.

EXERCISE

- Match the pairs of words above to their meanings below:

1. A small red or black insect that lives in a community.
   Your mother or father's sister.

2. Where two sides meet in a competition.
   When lots of people walk together with an intention.

3. Cooked pig, often served for lunch in sandwiches.
   Another word for damage.

4. A Chinese frying pan.
   Putting one foot in front of the other to move somewhere.

5. An early 20th century dance music.
   Glass containers where food is kept.

6. Number, one more than nine, one less than eleven.
   Verb, meaning to change direction

7. Adverb meaning frequently.
   A child whose parents are no longer alive.

8. A building in a farm where animals are kept.
   Another word for prohibition.

9. Past tense of the verb to shoot.
   Adjective, the opposite of long.

- Check your answers in the answer key.

Contractions | Structure

- Listen to the conversation below:

9.8 🎧

> A What's the time?
> B I don't know. I've left my watch at home.
> A Oh, I'll go and ask in that cafe.
> B They won't help you in there. They're very rude¡
> A Really? I should've charged my phone. I'm so disorganised¡

- Underline the words that have been shortened.
- Which words are shortened in English speech?

+ A contraction is where **two or more words are shortened**.
+ Words that contract are: have, be, would, will & not.
+ Contractions are **not normally written in English** except for those containing 'not'.
+ Contractions are pronounced as follows:

9.9 🎧 **HAVE**

- Contracts to /v/ after a vowel (I've, you've, we've).
- Contracts to /əv/ after a consonant (what've, should've).

HAS

- Follows the < s > endings rule (she's, it's).

BE

- 'are' contracts to /ə(r)/ in most cases (they're, we're).
- 'is' follows the < s > endings rule (Joe's, Kate's).

WILL

- Contracts to /l/ after vowels (I'll, you'll).
- Contracts to /əl/ after consonants (what'll, it'll)

NOT

- 'not' contracts to /nt/ in most cases (don't, shouldn't).
- can't is pronounced /kɑːnt/
- aren't is pronounced /ɑːnt/
- weren't is pronounced /wɜːnt/

EXERCISE

- Listen to the conversation and write in the missing contractions:

A [1]_____ John gone this evening?

B [2]_____ be working, [3]_____ he?

A Probably, he always is.

I [4]_____ asked him earlier.

B [5]_____ been lucky.

[6]_____ spent most of the day in bed, sleeping.

A [7]_____ right. [8]_____ so tired at the moment.

[9]_____ try not to worry though.

EXERCISE

i) Without listening to the recording, study the conversations and work out how the contractions in bold are pronounced

COFFEE

A Right. [1]**That'll** be five pounds eighty then, please.

B How much? You [2]**aren't** joking, are you?

A No, sir. [3]**You've** asked for two milky coffees, [4]**haven't** you?

B Yes, so how much is each one?

It [5]**can't** be nearly three pounds, surely?

A You [6]**haven't** visited London recently then sir!

[7]**That's** how much things cost these days!

PARKING

A Eh! You [1]**can't** park there. [1]**It's** a double yellow line.

B But [2]**I'll** only be two minutes. [3]**I've** got to pick up a parcel.

A I [4]**don't** care what you're doing. I [5]**won't** let you park there.

B [6]**I'm** in such a hurry. Please let me, [7]**it'll** make it so much easier!

A Oh, alright. Go on. But [8]**this'll** be the first and last time.

ii) Listen and check your answers then practise saying the conversations.

Stress Shift | Structure

- Listen to the word 'underneath' said alone then in a sentence:

9.13 🎧   "Underneath"

              "It's underneath the bookshelf."

- What do you notice about the stress in 'underneath' in each sentence?

+ Some constructions in spoken English are said with **different stress patterns** depending on the words surrounding them.
+ This is known as stress shift, and commonly occurs in the following:

9.14 🎧 ABBREVIATIONS

+ Stress normally occurs on the **first and last letter** of an abbreviation.
+ When followed by another word, the stress shifts **from the last letter** of the abbreviation **to the first**:

Examples	ˌBBˈC - ˌBBC ˈOne	ˌUˈK - ˌUK ˈCitizen

PHRASAL VERBS

+ Main stress normally occurs on the **particle**.
+ When a **content word is before or after** the particle, stress shifts:

Examples	ˌgo ˈup - ˌgo up the ˈstairs	ˌwrite ˈdown - ˌwrite the ˈpoem down

-TEEN NUMBERS

+ Main stress normally occurs on the suffix **-teen**.
+ Stress shifts **to the beginning** when followed by a content word:

Examples	thirˈteen - ˌthirteen specˈtators	ˌnineˈteen - ˌnineteen ˈpounds

3 SYLLABLE WORDS

+ If the main stress normally falls on the final syllable of a 3 syllable word, it will **shift to the first syllable** when followed by a content word:

Examples	ˌafterˈnoon - ˌafternoon ˈtea	ˌJapaˈnese - ˌJapanese ˈsailor

DRILL

- Repeat the -teen numbers then say them with the object on the recording.

13 14 15 16 17 18 19

EXERCISE

i) Match the organisations in column A with the abbreviations in B.
ii) Say the abbreviations with final-letter stress.
iii) Add a suitable noun from column C and move the stress to the noun:

EXAMPLE 'National Health Service' | ‚NH'S | ‚NHS 'Nurse

A	B	C
National Health Service	BP	nurse
British Petroleum	NHS	service station
Territorial Army	EU	hostel
Young Men's Christian Association	TA	member
United States of America	USA	president
European Union	YMCA	soldier

DRILL

Repeat the highlighted word using final syllable stress, then say the sentence shifting the stress to the first syllable:

1. **Canto'nese**   Let's have a cantonese wok.
2. **refe'ree**   The referee's assistant has signalled "off-side"
3. **pictur'esque**   What a picturesque village this is.
4. **million'aire**   Dave would love to be a millionaire sportsman.
5. **volun'teer**   As there were no police, they launched a volunteer rescue.
6. **Japan'ese**   I enjoy Japanese cinema greatly.

Adverbials | Intonation

- Listen to the opinions below:

9.18 🎧

"Frankly, I don't think they'll last a year."

"I'd have to agree with that, basically."

"Personally, I would never have put them together!"

"I think you're all jealous, to be honest."

- What do you notice about the intonation of the underlined words/phrases?

+ Adverbials are often used in spoken English to **restrict the meaning** of a sentence.
+ At the **beginning of a sentence or phrase**, they use fall-rise (↘↗) intonation.
+ At the **end of a sentence or phrase**, they use rising (↗) intonation.

DRILL

- Repeat the adverbials firstly with fall-rising, then rising intonation:

9.19 🎧

At the beginning ↘↗		At the end ↗
Basically		basically.
Frankly		frankly.
Actually		actually.
To be 'honest	sentence	to be 'honest.
Unfortunately		unfortunately.
Personally		personally.
As far as 'I'm concerned		as far as 'I'm concerned.
On the 'whole		on the 'whole.
If you ask 'me		if you ask 'me.

EXERCISE

- Match each adverbial in the box with a suitable phrase below, then say the phrase in two ways:

> i) with the adverbial at the beginning with fall-rise intonation
>
> ii) with the adverbial at the end and rise intonation.

> basically frankly actually to be honest unfortunately
> personally As far as I'm concerned on the whole if you ask me

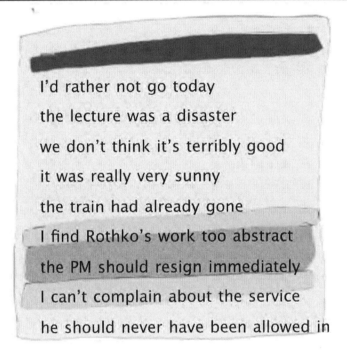

I'd rather not go today

the lecture was a disaster

we don't think it's terribly good

it was really very sunny

the train had already gone

I find Rothko's work too abstract

the PM should resign immediately

I can't complain about the service

he should never have been allowed in

- Listen to the answers and practise.

EXERCISE

- Listen to some conversations using adverbials.
- Create some of your own examples that you can use in your everyday speech.

Phrasal Verb Stress | Postscript

- Listen to the following sentences:

9.22 🎧

"Hand it over!"

"Hand the money over!"

- Where is the main stress in each case?

+ Phrasal verbs (verb + particle) **normally place stress on the particle**.
+ If a content word appears near the particle **either before or after**, it will take the stress from the particle.

EXERCISE

- In each example, underline the main stress.

1. "let in"
>   i) "Let me <u>in</u>!"
>   ii) "Can you let <u>George</u> in?"

2. "finish off"
>   i) I can't believe you finished off the chocolate!
>   ii) I'll be with you in a minute, I'm just finishing off.

3. "write down"
>   i) Could you write this address down?
>   ii) I've forgotten your number, can I write it down?

4. "throw away"
>   i) This dress is horrible, I'm going to throw it away.
>   ii) Why did you throw the television away?

5. "give out"
>   i) "Why are these leaflets here? Didn't you give them out?
>   ii) "John, could you give these sheets out?"

9.23 🎧   - Listen and check your answers.

Answer Key

Consonant Articulation I Sounds

EXERCISE
1. f/v   2. t/d/l/n   3. m/p/b   4. k/g/ŋ   5. θ/ð   6. h/?

EXERCISE
- sentence 2 'Who took Paul's watch' uses only rounded vowels.

Introduction I Spelling & Sound

EXERCISE
1. choose   2. lose   3. played   4. author   5. said   6. put   7. gone   8. food   9. slow
10. worn   11. wall

Schwa I Spelling & Sound

- around /əˈraʊnd/, manner /ˈmænə/, sailor /ˈseɪlə/, cactus /ˈkæktəs/
- /ə/ appears in every IPA transcription (in bold above).

EXERCISE

servant persist bacon picture commit alive
jumper sublime London salad Peru structure
suggest soldier persuade combine balloon
terror cushion scripture tighten sofa Russia

Function & Content I Structure

- 'go' and 'walk' are stressed because they carry meaning.
- The other words 'shall', 'we', 'for', & 'a' are all grammatical words used to gel the sentence.

EXERCISE
1. Can we go for a swim in the sea?
2. It's a beautiful day in the South of England.
3. How do you want to pay for this sir?
4. Jessica Smith is required in 'Arrivals' immediately.
5. When you get to the station, give me a call.
6. Would you like some of my carrot cake?

Schwa Function Words I Structure

- Function words pronounced with schwa in the passage: 'to', 'for', 'a', 'of', 'but', 'the', 'are', 'there', 'a', 'have', 'at'.

Introduction I Intonation

- i) 'Maybe' = ↘↗yes   ii) 'Definitely' = ↘yes   iii) 'Why are you asking?' = ↗yes.

EXERCISE

1. ↘   2. ↘↗   3. ↗   4. ↗   5. ↘   6. ↘↗

Usage I Intonation

EXERCISE

1. ATTITUDE

i) In the first version, the father is excited and interested, in the second he is uninterested and a little rude.

ii) The father's intonation is falling in both examples, the main difference is that he starts from a much higher pitch in the first example. This shows more emotion. In the second version, he starts his phrase quite low, showing disinterest.

2. IMPLICATION

i) In the first version, we understand that person B really felt the film was good. In the second version, he is not entirely sure, he is showing reservation, we are expecting him to say something less positive now.

ii) In the first version, person B uses falling intonation on 'it was good', whereas in the second version he uses fall-rising intonation, known as an implicational fall-rise.

3. REPETITION

- The first question is asking for new information, person A does not know the answer and uses falling intonation. The second time she asks, she already knows the answer, she is repeating the question and for this reason uses rising intonation.

IPA I Postscript

- The IPA version shows us a silent < r >, a long vowel /:/ and a silent < a >. It also indicates the pronunciation of the vowels /ə/ and /i/.

EXERCISE

1	autumn	ɔ:təm	n
2	half	hɑ:f	l
3	lamb	læm	b
4	know	nəʊ	k (and w)
5	island	aɪlənd	s
6	light	laɪt	gh
7	cupboard	ˈkʌbəd	p (and r)
8	write	raɪt	w
9	often	ɒfən	t
10	handbag	hænbæg	d

< th > I Sound Comparison

- /θ/ is a **voiceless** sound; it only aqueezing air past the teeth.
- /ð/ is a **voiced** sound, the throat vibrates whilst air is pushed past the teeth.
- Everything else iin the two sounds is the same - the place of articulation is **dental** and they are both **fricative** consonants.

EXERCISE

θ	ð
South, both, thought, thank, bath, fifths, author, mouth, months	Southern, this, the, those, bathe, baths, rather, mouths, soothe

RULES
- Most content words are pronounced with /θ/ - South, thought, both, thought, thank, bath, fifths, author, mouth, months
- All function words are pronounced with /ð/ - this, the, those,
- Verbs ending <the> are pronounced with /ð/ - bathe, soothe
- Plural words ending < vowel + ths > are pronounced /ð/ - baths, mouths
- Plural words ending < consonant + ths > are pronounced /θ/ - fifths, months
- Words containing < ther > are pronounced /ð/ - rather, Southern

EXERCISE - Odd Word Out
1. mouths   2. author   3. those   4. clothes   5. thin

EXERCISE - Word Grid
bother - breathe - these - leather - father - Southern - other - those - together - rhythm - feather - although

< s > Endings I Spelling & Sound

- Why's (< s > pronounced /z/), Matt's (< s > pronounced /s/), badges (< s > pronounced /ɪz/)
- Why's (< s > added as a contraction of 'is'), Matt's (< s > added to show possession), badges (< s > added to make the plural).

/s/	/z/	/ɪz/
tops, tanks, wants, laughs, surfs, creates, alerts, looks, cracks, interests	hands, lobs, begs, returns, loves, answers, prays, prefers, seems, climbs,	chooses, misses, faxes, chases, amazes, pushes, inches, matches, ages, badges,

EXERCISE - Odd Word Out
1. devastates   2. traces   3. fails   4. drags   5. talks   6. places

Schwa I Structure
- 'There are a few of them' contains 5 schwa sounds /ðər ər ə fju: əv ðəm/

5. What <u>have</u> I done <u>to the</u> dinner?
6. <u>Shall</u> you <u>and</u> I ask <u>her</u>?
7. <u>Do</u> they think <u>that</u> we will?

EXERCISE - Circle the bold words if they are pronounced with schwa.
The bold word should be circled in the following sentences:
1. A   2. B   3. A   4. A   5. A   6. A   7. A   8. A   9. B

Sentence Stress I Intonation

- 'What', 'like', 'cup' and 'tea' are stressed.
- The strongest stressed words are 'like' and 'tea' because they are at the end of the sentences.

EXERCISE - Match the Words.
A pair of shoes.   A pint of milk.   A leg of lamb.   A bunch of flowers.   A bag of crisps.
A glass of wine.   A book of poems.   A joint of beef.   A loaf of bread.

Tonic Syllable I Intonation

Most stressed words are:
A 'buy',
B 'going'
A 'bag'
B 'trousers'

EXERCISE
- Circle the Content Words:
four,   two,   art,   wife,   half,   use,   sum,   sheet,   sorting,   wood
- Underline the last content word:
1. want   2. laugh   3. give   4. wanted   5. like   6. see   7. have   8. card   9. money
10. fun

Homographs I Postscript

/riːd/ and /red/ are both written as 'read' in this case.

EXERCISE
1. close   2. lead   3. number   4. tear   5. wind   6. rows

Long Vowels I Sounds

- English speakers often say /ɜː/ when they are thinking. In writing, this may be spelt 'er', for example 'errrr, I'm not sure......'

EXERCISE

iː	uː	ɜː	ɔː	ɑː
dream cheek grief Chinese evening beast	Tuesday clue spoon suit food threw	curse word thirty church earth worth	jaw walk horse door brought quarter	half park father last shark car

ɪ vs iː I Sound Comparison

- 'sit' is pronounced /ɪ/, 'seat' is pronounced /siːt/. The most important difference between the two sounds is the position of the mouth - /ɪ/ is lower and more neutral than /iː/. There is a slight difference in length, with /iː/ being slightly longer in this case.

EXERCISE

1. did / deed   2. chip / cheap   3. rid / read   4. fist / feast   5. itch / each   6. grin / green
7. chick / cheek   8. live / leave   9. pick / peak   10. sick / seek

EXERCISE

1. a) chip b) cheap   2. a) green b) grin   3. a) each b) itch   4. a) leave b) live
5. a) pick b) peak   6. a) rid b) read

< r > I Spelling & Sound

- butter /bʌtə/ - does not contain a pronounced /r/
- bread /bred/ - contains a pronounced /r/

EXERCISE
1. heart   2. world (or earth)   3. door   4. turkey   5. flower   6. shirt   7. four   8. guitar
9. chair

EXERCISE
Names that contain silent < r >: Heather, Shirly, Carla, Burt, Charlotte, Kirsty,

EXERCISE
father - learn - horse - Berlin - fork - Turkey - important - harder - sport - sharp - birthday - water - warm - Barcelona - poor - first - burn - perfect - Liverpool - New York - Manchester

Two Syllable Words | Structure

X .	. X
angle awful bishop carpet father foolish pardon English candle lettuce orphan sofa turtle	alive appeal beside balloon commit decide delete erase forbid involve machine persuade release revise survive

EXERCISE
1. parade   2. conquer   3. amaze   4. canal   5. machine   6. police

Wh- Questions | Intonation

- In the first question, the intonation is falling because the speaker does not know the answer.
- In the second question, the intonation is rising, the speaker already knows the answer and is repeating the question.

EXERCISE
1. a) ↗ b) ↘   2. a) ↗ b) ↘   3. a) ↘ b) ↗   4. a) ↘ b) ↗   5. a) ↘ b) ↗

6. a) ↗ b) ↘   7. a) ↘ b) ↗

Homophones | Postscript

- The words are 'aren't' and 'aunt'. Their pronunciation is identical.

EXERCISE
i)
1. a) air b) heir   2. a) bored b) board   3. a) dear b) deer   4. a) flour b) flower
5. a) jeans b) genes
ii)
court / caught   father / farther   nose / knows   none / nun   sew / so   sun / son
through / threw   war / wore   warn / worn   weather / whether   build / billed   which/witch

t vs ? I Sound Comparison

- 'football' does not contain a pronounced /t/. The < t > is instead normally pronounced as a glottal stop /?/.
- the words 'foot' and 'footer' both contain a pronounced /t/.

EXERCISE
2. Many regional accents of English use a glottal stop /?/ before weak vowels (water) and at the end of words (heat). The most famous example of this is Cockney, but most other regional accents behave in a similar way.

EXERCISE
1. waiter   2. butler   3. Saturn   4. atmosphere   5. waterfall

EXERCISE
1. a) ? b) t   2. a) ? b) t   3. a) t b) ?   4. a) t b) ?   5. a) ? b) t

< ed > endings I Spelling & Sound

- in 'chopped' < ed > is pronounced /t/.
- in 'boiled' < ed > is pronounced /d/.
- in roasted < ed > is pronounced /ɪd/.

EXERCISE
stated ɪd   looked t   argued d   dubbed d   capped t   interested ɪd   deleted ɪd
sipped t   sacked t   annoyed d   chewed d   rated ɪd   shifted ɪd   retired d   faced t
blinded ɪd   flashed t   loved d   ended ɪd   pushed t   decided ɪd   climbed d
headed ɪd   inched t   surfed t   pulled d   answered d   intruded ɪd

EXERCISE
A killed   B rated   C addressed   D closed   E deepened   F joked

3 Syllable Words I Structure

- manager /ˈmænədʒə/ = first syllable stress.
- banana /bəˈnɑːnə/ = second syllable stress.
- entertain /ˌentəˈteɪn/ = third syllable stress with secondary stress on the first syllable.

EXERCISE
1. poˈlitely   2. ˈrelative   3. ˈpassionate   4. ˈinterested   5. Jaˈmaica   6. lecturer

EXERCISE

X..	.X.	x.X
politics happily satisfied clarify credible quality octopus energy funeral ignorant wonderful syllable	supporter believer courageous prevention tomorrow annoying amusement adventure reaction abolish consider	kangaroo afternoon Portuguese Japanese underneath seventeen cigarette picturesque serviette recommend refugee volunteer

Yes/No Questions | Intonation

A Have you seen the time? FALL-RISING
B No, are we late? RISING
A Yes! Don't you have a watch? RISING
B No, but I have a phone. Could you pass it to me? FALL-RISING

A Hello madam, Inspector Hombs. May I ask you some questions? RISING
B Yes, go ahead.
A Were you at home last night? FALLING
B Yes, why? Has something happened? RISING

- All the questions except 'why?' could be answered with 'yes' or 'no'.
- All three intonation patterns: rising, fall-rising and falling are used.

EXERCISE
1. ↗ 2. ↘↗ 3. ↘ 4. ↘↗ 5. ↗ 6. ↘ 7. ↗ 8. ↘↗

Silent Syllables | Postscript

ACROSS
1. miserable   2. several   3. opera   4. police   5. dictionary   6. laboratory   7. history
8. chocolate   9. average

DOWN
1. aspirin   2. separate   3. restaurant   4. conference   5. mineral   6. interesting
7. family

- The grey squares are vowels that are normally silent in pronunciation.

Short Vowels I Sounds

- 'Jim's good friend's duck ran off' contains 6 vowels, each of them is short, and none is repeated.

EXERCISE

ɪ	ʊ	e	ʌ	æ	ɒ
kick quick grill shift chip wrist	pull could bush look would butcher	test fence pleasure ready send leisure	trust company thorough mother hunt bug	cash bag fashion value ran add	dog watch shop wrong wander problem

/h/ I Sounds

- We make the sound /h/ when we steam up a mirror.
- This sound comes from the glottis, in the throat.

< h > in Function Words I Structure

- In 'What's he doing' the < h > in 'he' is not pronounced.
- In 'He's having lunch I think' the < he > in 'he' is pronounced.

EXERCISE
A Where's he gone?
B He said he was going to the bank.

A What does her brother do?
B Her brother? He's a plumber.

A How am I going to break the news to him?
B Sit him down, give him a cup of tea and explain slowly.

A Have we got a map in here?
B Oh no, we must have left it at home.

A What's his name?
B His first name's David, but I've forgotten his surname.

Silent Letters I Spelling & Sound

- sword   lamb   island   castle

EXERCISE
1. answer   2. dumb   3. handbag   4. ghost   5. foreign   6. listen   7. knit   8. yolk
9. wrong   10. sign   11. dawn   12. postman

Joining Introduction | Structure

- 'didn't_you' is joined with /tʃ/ (didəntʃu)
- 'you_offer' is joined with /w/ (juwɒfə)
- 'offer_Anne' is joined with /r/ (ɒfəræn)
- 'Anne_Ball' is joined with /m/ (æmbɔːl)
- 'Ball_lunch' is joined with one long /l/ (bɔːlʌntʃ)

EXERCISE
i)
1. What_a lot_of nonsense
2. It_isn't_at_all bad
3. Can_I take_an_apple?
4. I fell_in love_on holiday.
5. Her bank_account_is_in the red.
6. It's_a bit_of_a joke

iii)
Words/phrases that assimilate are:
1. handbag   2. Batman   3. grand party   4. London Buses   5. down below
6. red car   7. one metre

Prominence | Intonation

'Do you like pizza?' - 'pizza' is most stressed because it is the last new content word.
'I like all Italian food.' - 'all' is most stressed because it is the last **new** content word. In this context both 'Italian' and 'food' are old because we are already talking about 'pizza'.

EXERCISE
1. scared   2. Bush   3. three   4. Mercedes   5. four   6. white   7. Spain   8. never
9. chips   10. allowed

Verb/Noun Stress Shift | Postscript

'I'd like a refund for these trousers' - 'refund is a noun with first syllable stress.
'I'm afraid we don't refund items over 28...' - 're'fund' is a verb with second syllable stress.

EXERCISE
ii)
1. a) 'research b) re'search   2. a) ob'ject b) 'object   3. a) pro'gress b) 'progress
4. a) 'permitt b) per'mitt   5. a) 'increase b) in'crease   6. a) pre'sent b) 'present

Weak ɪ vs ə I Sound Comparison

- 'chicken' /tʃɪkɪn/ does not contain a schwa sound.
- 'beaten' /biːtən/, 'driven' /drɪvən/, and 'children' /tʃɪldrən/ all contain schwa sounds.

EXERCISE

ə	ɪ
accent fossil Thomas evil China madness persuade council Japan danger garden lentil England parade spoken pencil	erase kitchen explain manage orange purchase kisses return bandage harvest demand English misses believe wicked defence turning surface

Weak i vs ɪ I Sound Comparison

- 'taxes' is pronounced /tæksɪz/
- 'taxis' is pronounced /tæksiz/
- The only difference between the are the weak forms /ɪ/ and /i/.

EXERCISE
1. i = he, ɪ = with, this, carpet
2. i = Mandy, ɪ = meeting, this, evening
3. i = She's, Burnley, ɪ = visiting
4. i = we, really, whiskey, ɪ = Did, finish
5. i = Katie, me, we, sushi, ɪ = is, with
6. i = Johnny, nearly, me,
7. i = he, really, ɪ = did, inconsiderate, him

< oo > I Spelling & Sound

- 4 different vowel sounds are produced: 'look' /lʊk/, 'flood' /flʌd/, 'poor' /pɔː/, 'moon' /muːn/.

ʊ	uː	ʌ	ɔː
stood wood book shook took wool brook cook foot good look rook hood hook	troop fool food soon cool roof smooth zoom balloon shampoo zoo tooth room	blood flood	moor poor floor door

EXERCISE
cook - foot - good - hood - wool - blood - stood - door - flood - look - took - shook - woof - floor

Vowel + Vowel Joining I Structure

- 'free us' joins with a /j/.
- 'Lisa Adams' joins with a /r/.
- 'Go out' joins with a /w/.

EXERCISE

j	w	r
Can you see it? I'll bring your tray up in a minute. Fry it in a little oil. The day after tomorrow. Can we buy a new toaster? A toy elephant. I feel free as a bird.	Joe isn't here. The two of you will win! That's so exciting! How about a tea? You'll get through it. Who are you? Now and then.	Can you hear it? They're mother and daughter. Are we near Oxford? No sir I can't help. It's the law of averages. Can you spare a minute?

Question Tags I Intonation

- '↘ aren't you?' Is a falling question tag, it is a statement, the speaker knows the answer.
- '↗ aren't you?' Is a rising question tag, it is a question, the speaker is not sure.

EXERCISE
- The mother uses falling intonation in tags 1 - 5 because she is making statements. She is not really asking her son, the effect is more that she is telling him.
- The mother uses rising intonation in tag 6 because she wants to receive a genuine answer from her son.

EXERCISE
- ↗ 'are you' is a question, the speaker is not sure.

- ↘ 'do you' is a statement, the speaker can see that the person does not recognise her.
- ↗ 'don't you' is a question, the speaker is not sure.

- ↗ 'have you' is a question.

- ↗ 'isn't it' is a question.

'have' I Postscript

- 'have' is pronounced in 4 different ways in the dialogue.

EXERCISE

What **have** you got planned for this evening? /əv/
I **have** to work on my thesis. /hæf/
That's a shame. We're going to **have** sushi in the centre. /hæv/
Have you tried sushi before? /həv/
No, but the others **have**. Have you? /hæv/
I might **have** done once, ages ago. /əv/
Well, we'll **have** to go out another night. /hæf/
Absolutely, **have** fun. /hæv/

Diphthongs I Sound Comparison

EXERCISE

	eɪ	ɔɪ	aɪ	əʊ	aʊ	ɪə	eə
b	bay	boy	buy	bow	bow	beer	bear
d	day		die dye	dough		deer dear	dare
m	may		my	mow		mere	mayor mare
p	pay		pie			peer pier	pair pear
r	ray		rye	row	row	rear	rare
s	say	soy	sigh	so sew sow		sear	
t		toy	tie Thai	tow		tear tier	tear
w	way		why		wow		wear where

EXERCISE
1. gɪə   2. bəʊt   3. keɪk   4. kɔɪn   5. saɪn   6. aʊl   7. tʃeə

< o > I Spelling & Sound

- Who's = /uː/   stolen = /əʊ/   son's = /ʌ/   boxing = /ɒ/   gown = /aʊ/

ɒ	ʌ	əʊ	uː	aʊ
long cod log cross shot dock	month tongue front shove some love	comb bold alone so cold low	move do lose tomb prove who	how down now cow allow brown

EXERCISE

gone - done - owl - so - son - wolf - women - brown - nothing - grown - not - do - chop - lose - port - rope - show - love - FINISH

Compounds I Structure

- In each word, the main stress is on the first syllable.

EXERCISE

- granddad, **telephone call**, grandma, newspapers, anything, boyfriend,
  engagement ring, **wedding bells**.
- Those above in **bold** are two separate words.
EXERCISE

ironing board, coat hanger, rocking chair, laptop, teapot, bookshelf, candlestick holder,
dining table, microwave (oven), lampshade, flower pot.

High Fall I Intonation

- The first time, person B seems to really mean what they are saying and appears to be
  excited about it.
- The second time, person B sounds less interested, possibly sarcastic, as if they are
  saying the opposite to their words.

EXERCISE

I haven't seen you for ages! - Information
It was in London, wasn't it? - Statement Question Tag
at the old friends' reunion. - Information
how are things? - Information Question
Pretty good! - Exclamation
I've been working on a new book. - Information
What's this one about? - Information Question
It's a biography of a sixteenth century scientist. - Information
How interesting! - Exclamation
When will it be finished? - Information Question
And how have you been? - Information Question
You didn't hear, did you? - Statement Question Tag
Katie had a baby last year! - Information
A little boy. - Information
Amazing! - Exclamation
You're a father! - Exclamation
Congratulations! - Exclamation
Who would have thought it? - Information Question
I can't quite believe it myself. Information
What's his name? Information Question
Peter. - Information
Peter's a lovely name. - Information
Listen I must be off! - Information
I have a train to catch. - Information
We must meet up soon. - Information
Absolutely. - Exclamation
I'll give you a call. - Information.

'do' I Postscript

i) dəʊnt ii) də iii) du: iv) du:wɪŋ v) dʒu

EXERCISE
1. də 2. dʒu 3. du: dəʊnt 4. du: 5. dəʊnt 6. də 7. du:

Nasal Assimilations I Sounds

EXERCISE

ii)

First Name	Anne (m)	Karen (ŋ)	Ben (n)	Aaron (ŋ)	Lauren (ŋ)
Surname	Peters	Cole	Lane	Carter	Grove
First Name	John (m)	Ken (n)	Sean (m)	Jane (n)	Wayne (m)
Surname	Bates	Edwards	Bailey	Thomas	Mayfield

iii)
1. Have you bee**n(m)** playi**ng(ŋ)** o**n(ŋ)** Katie's computer agai**n(n)**?
2. Wi**n(ŋ)** cars, wi**n(m)** money an**d(n)** wi**n(m)** big prizes tonigh**t(n)**!
3. O**n(m)** paper the ba**n(ŋ)** could work, but i**n(n)** reality it wo**n't(n)**.
4. Ca**n(n)** I have a thi**n(m)** piece of Belgia**n(ŋ)** cake?
5. I'll telepho**ne(n)** you whe**n(m)** my so**n(ŋ)** ca**n(ŋ)** come.

ŋ vs ŋg I Sound Comparison

- 'singer' /sɪŋə/ does not contain a /g/ sound.
- 'single' /sɪŋgəl/ and 'finger' /fɪŋgə/ both contain a /g/ sound.

EXERCISE

ŋ	ŋg
taxing thing sting working wing bang wrongly movingly singer	finger hunger England Hungary stronger longer mango tango single angle

i) < ng > is pronounced /ŋ/ at the end of a word.
ii) < ng > is pronounced /ŋg/ in superlatives and comparatives.
iii) < ng > is pronounced /ŋg/ when it appears in the middle of a word, except when an ending has been added to a root ending < ng >.

EXERCISE
1. Bangladesh   2. hung   3. young   4. along   5. speaking   6. hanger   7. wrongly
8. ringing   9. slang   10. strong

< a > I Spelling & Sound

- 8 different vowel sounds are produced:
/ɒ/ wanted, /ɔː/ raw, /ə/ tuna, /eɪ/ Dave & waiter, /ɑː/ asked, /eə/ rare, /ɪ/ village, /æ/ lamb.

EXERCISE
wasp, atlas, safe, spare, rat, shark, half, what, chase, ask, salt, watch, gate, hat, talk, schwa, saw, was

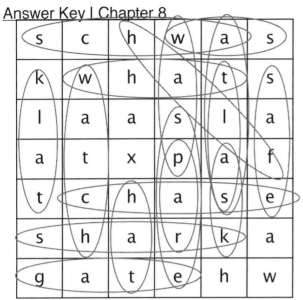

s	c	h	w	a	s
k	w	h	a	t	s
l	a	a	s	l	a
a	t	x	p	a	f
t	c	h	a	s	e
s	h	a	r	k	a
g	a	t	e	h	w

Name Compounds I Structure

- 'Oxford Street' uses only first word stress.
- 'Cambridge Road', 'Regent's Park' & 'Church Way' stress both words.

EXERCISE
First Element Stress: Goodge Street, Cannon Street, Bond Street, Liverpool Street.

EXERCISE
1. Eric Jones, Clifton Gardens   2. Jane Michaels, Fenchurch Street

Material & Ingredient Compounds I Structure

- 'pear tart' (double stress), 'carrot cake' (first element stress).

EXERCISE
1. apple tart   2. potato cake   3. woolen jumper   4. glass cabinet   5. dinner jacket
6. banana smoothie

Implicational Fall-rise I Intonation

- In the second version of each conversation, person B uses an implicational fall-rise. The
  meaning changes to 'maybe', or 'not completely'.

EXERCISE
1. a) ↘ b) ↘↗   2. a) ↘↗ b) ↘   3. a) ↘↗ b) ↘   4. a) ↘ b) ↘↗   5. a) ↘↗ b) ↘

'are' I Postscript

- 4 different pronunciations (in order): ə, ɑːnt, ɑː, ər.

EXERCISE
(in order) ər, ə, ɑː, ə, ə, ɑːnt.

tʃ & dʒ Assimilations | Sounds

- 4 affricates are pronounced: 'did you' /dɪdʒu/, 'try' /tʃraɪ/, 'drinks' /dʒrɪŋks/, 'Tuesday' /tʃu:zdeɪ/
- Each could be pronounced differently: /dɪd ju/, /traɪ/, /drɪŋks/, /tju:zdeɪ/

EXERCISE
1. Would you like to hear my tune?
2. When did your train arrive?
3. Draw a tree in the background.
4. The box had 'Europe' traced onto its lid.
5. Do you know how to drive?
6. Might your tulips flower this month?
7. The duke is coming for lunch this Tuesday.
8. There's a bit of a draft, could you close the window?
9. Aren't you coming to the studio?
10. I'm sorry, I just don't trust you.

Long vs Short Vowels | Sound Comparison

EXERCISE
i)

	æ	ɑ:	ɒ	ɔ:	e	ʌ	ɜ:
b__t	bat			bought	bet	but	
p__t	pat	part	pot	port	pet	putt	pert
t__n	tan			torn	ten	ton	turn
h__t	hat	heart	hot			hut	hurt
k__t	cat	cart	cot	caught/ court		cut	curt
b__d	bad	barred		bored/ board	bed	bud	bird
w__k	whack		wok	walk			work
b__n	ban	barn		born		bun	burn

ii)
hæt, hɑ:t, bɜ:d, wɔ:k, kʌt, pɒt, bed

EXERCISE
1. ant / aunt   2. match / march   3. ham / harm   4. wok / walk   5. jazz / jars
6. ten / turn   7. often / orphan   8. barn / ban   9. shot / short

Contractions I Spelling & Sound

- <u>what's</u> <u>don't</u> <u>I've</u> <u>I'll</u> <u>won't</u> <u>they're</u> <u>should've</u> <u>I'm</u>
- Auxiliary verbs be, have, will and would are often shortened. So is the word 'not'.

EXERCISE
1. Where's 2. He'll 3. Won't 4. should've 5. You'd've 6. He's 7. That's 8. He's
9. I'll

EXERCISE
COFFEE 1. ðætəl 2. ɑːnt 3. juv 4. hævənt 5. kɑːnt 6. hævənt 7. ðæts
PARKING 1. kɑːnt 2. ɪts 3. aɪv 4. dəʊnt 5. wəʊnt 6. aɪm 7. ɪtəl 8. ðɪsəl

Stress Shift I Structure

- In 'Underneath' the stress is on the last syllable 'neath'.
- In 'It's underneath the bookshelf', the stress is on 'under'.

EXERCISE
National Health Service, NHS, nurse
British Petroleum, BP, service station
Territorial Army, TA, soldier
Young Men's Christian Association, YMCA, hostel
United State's of America, USA, president
European Union, EU, member

Adverbials I Intonation

- Those at the beginning, 'Frankly' and 'Personally' use fall-rising intonation.
- Those at the end, 'basically' and 'to be honest' use rising intonation.

EXERCISE
Use the recording for the answers and intonation.

Phrasal Verb Stress I Postscript

- In 'Hand it over' the main stress is on 'over'.
- In 'Hand the money over' the main stress is on 'money'.

EXERCISE
1. i) in ii) George 2. i) chocolate ii) off 3. i) address ii) down 4. i) away ii) television
5. i) out ii) sheets

Glossary

adverbial - A word or phrase that functions like an adverb e.g. 'basically'.

affricate - A single sound that combines a plosive followed immediately by a fricative.

alveolar ridge - The hard gum behind the upper teeth.

approximant - A vowel-like consonant sound made without fully blocking air.

articulation - The action involved in producing a sound.

articulator - Part of the mouth or throat used to block or shape air to form sounds.

assimilation - When a consonant sound changes due to the following consonant.

consonant - Type of sound made by blocking air as it leaves the body.

compound - Word or phrase formed of two or more words which create a new meaning combined.

content word - A word that has a specific meaning such as a noun, main verb, adjective or adverb.

contraction - When two or more words join together and shorten.

diphthong - A single vowel sound made by starting in one position and moving to another.

ending - Letters added to an existing word (root) to change its meaning or type.

fricative - A consonant sound where air is squeezed through a blockage, sounding like friction.

function - Grammatical words (normally short) which 'glue' the sentence rather than carrying specific meaning.

glottal stop - A plosive consonant made by stopping the flow of air fully in the glottis.

glottis - An articulator found in the throat, containing the vocal cords.

homograph - Two or more words written identically but pronounced differently.

homophone - Two or more words pronounced identically but written differently.

IPA - International Phonetic Alphabet which contains symbols representing sounds.

labial - Place of articulation involving the lips.

monophthong - Vowel sound made using one position of the mouth.

nasal - Consonant sound released through the nose.

phrasal verb - A phrase made when a verb and another word combine to create a new meaning, e.g. 'bring up'.

plosive - Consonant sound made when airflow is fully blocked then released.

primary stress - The main stress in a word, marked /'/ in dictionaries, e.g. /'family/.

root - The basic word before an ending or prefix is added to it.

schwa - Weak vowel sound /ə/.

secondary stress - A level of stress weaker than primary in a word, marked /ˌ/ in dictionaries, e.g. /ˌunder'stand/.

stress - Making a sound strong through volume, pitch and possibly length.

stress pattern - A combination of stressed and unstressed syllables.

stress shift - Where stress moves to a different syllable from where it would normally be expected.

strong form - The form of a function word with a level of stress higher than weak.

syllable - A unit of pronunciation, normally containing a vowel sound, e.g. 'to-ge-ther' contains three syllables.

tonic syllable - The most stressed syllable in any sentence or phrase.

velum (adj. velar) - Place of articulation on the roof of the mouth at the back, behind the palate.

voiced - Sounds made vibration in the voice box; all vowels and many consonants are voiced.

voiceless - Sounds made without vibration in the voice box (through releasing only air).

vowel - Sound made through shaping the tongue, lips and jaw as air passes through.

weak form - Reduced form of a function word said with minimum level of stress.

ACKNOWLEDGEMENTS

A big thank you to all those associated with Pronunciation Studio London over the last few years, in no particular order: Tom Wisniowski, Lis Carter, Zainab Tapas, Farida Alvarez, David Bauckham, Erica Buist, Shanti Ulfsbjorninn, Chris Miller, Anne Walsh, Egle Karmonaite, Stuart Morrison, Simone Dietrich, Aminah Otmani & Cris Chatterjee; I have learnt an awful lot working with you.

Special thanks to Rayen La Penna & her eye for design, to Carlos Pachon Gonzalez for his work on the recordings and to Dan White for the 'Mister Schwa' cartoons.

FURTHER READING

Recommended books on the subject of phonetics and pronunciation are listed below:

Gimson, Alan Cruttenden. **Gimson's Pronunciation of English**. Hodder Arnold

International Phonetic Association: **Handbook of the International Phonetic Association**. Cambridge University Press

Roach, Peter. **English Phonetics & Phonology: A Practical Course.** Cambridge University Press

Wells, John. **English Intonation.** Cambridge University Press

Wells, John. **Longman Pronunciation Dictionary.** Pearson Longman.

THE AUTHOR

Joseph Hudson (BA/CELTA/IPA Cert) is a teacher and writer based in London. He founded the Pronunciation Studio Speech school in 2007. His early career was as a general English teacher, where he learnt the rudiments of language learning. He is the author of the courses 'An English Accent' and 'The Sound of English'.

THE RECORDINGS

The audio pack features the voice of Erica Buist (BA/CELTA/IPA Cert) alongside the author. Erica is an experienced and vibrant classroom teacher. She has taught general English and pronunciation in Central America and England and joined the Pronunciation Studio in 2009. Her voice skills are notably clear and warm.

THE SCHOOL

Pronunciation Studio London provides education in all aspects of speech from phonetics, pronunciation and accent reduction to voice coaching and acting classes. Over 10,000 students have passed through its doors since 2007. Creative teaching, exciting materials, a passion for language learning in general and phonetics in particular are central to its popularity.

Visit the Pronunciation Studio at www.pronunciationlondon.co.uk.

www.thesoundofenglish.org